Eduard Munk, William Yorke Fausset

The Student's Cicero

Adapted from the German of Dr. Munk's 'Geschichte der römischen Literatur'

Eduard Munk, William Yorke Fausset

The Student's Cicero
Adapted from the German of Dr. Munk's 'Geschichte der römischen Literatur'

ISBN/EAN: 9783337205997

Printed in Europe, USA, Canada, Australia, Japan

Cover: Foto ©ninafisch / pixelio.de

More available books at **www.hansebooks.com**

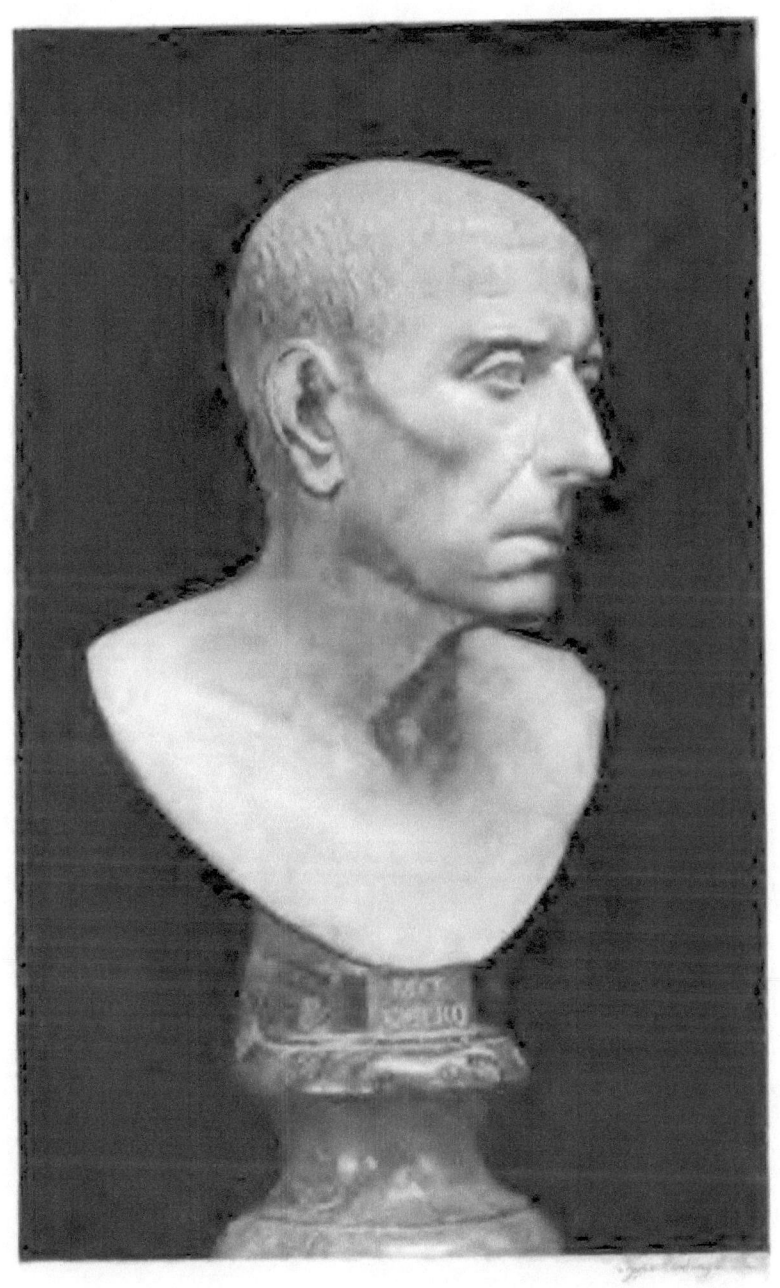

From the bust in the Uffizi Gallery Florence

THE
STUDENT'S CICERO

ADAPTED FROM THE GERMAN OF DR. MUNK'S
"GESCHICHTE DER RÖMISCHEN LITERATUR"

BY

THE REV. W. Y. FAUSSET, M.A.

OF FETTES COLLEGE, EDINBURGH

Editor of Cicero *Pro Cluentio*

With a Frontispiece Portrait

LONDON
SWAN SONNENSCHEIN & CO.
PATERNOSTER SQUARE
1889

PRINTED BY
CHAS. STRAKER AND SONS, BISHOPSGATE AVENUE, LONDON;
AND REDHILL.

PREFACE.

THIS little book is a translation of the Section devoted to Cicero in the first volume of Dr. Munk's *Geschichte der Römischen Literatur*. It is a literary biography of the great master of Latin prose, who wielded his eloquence in a Rome which, in spite of Greek influences and a tottering Republic, was still Roman and free.

Nor can the literary life of Cicero be dissociated from his public activity. Like some great statesmen of our own century, he found in literary labours a rest from politics; and he might have applied to himself the words of Africanus the elder, "that he was never less at leisure than when he had nothing to do."* It is doubtful whether Cicero himself would have allowed that literary work at its best is separable from practical life. His philosophical treatises seem to do scant justice to the purely theoretical virtues; in his rhetorical treatises the practical qualifications and task of the orator are largely dwelt on.† The speeches of Cicero were written to be heard, not read: the same fact accounts for the exquisite lucidity of his style.

Dr. Munk has done well in collecting so much ancient testimony to the unique position which Cicero held among Roman writers, together with such unfavourable criticism as antiquity affords. It is not difficult to lay one's finger on the weak points of his style and his character; on the diffuseness of the one, the transparent egotism of the other. Tried by our modern standard of taste and even of honour, he may sometimes be found guilty of failings to which no public man would now like to confess. We do not, for example, like to find him asking Lucceius to invest the doings of his consulship with more distinction than the strict laws of historical truth would allow.‡ In politics we know that he played a vacillating part, though it may be questioned whether it is fair to call him a "political trimmer."

But when Mommsen calls him "a dabbler, abounding in words, poor beyond all conception in ideas; nothing but an

---

* de off. iii. 1.   † E g. de orat. i. § 202.   ‡ ad fam. v. 12.

advocate and not a good one," we feel that it is well to go back to antiquity and ask whether there any anticipation of such a view is to be found. There is practically none; and Mommsen can only reply that the extravagant panegyrics of Caesar and Catullus* were rendered to the stylist Cicero, not to the author, still less to the statesman. Now to say nothing of the question whether the style can be thus separated from the man, whence came this marvellous fascination of style? For however the modern critic may exalt the Attic school of Calvus and the rest at the expense of Cicero, it is Cicero who has survived. Perhaps we may single out, among other excellences, the moral dignity of the Ciceronian style. St. Augustine tells us that it was the *Hortensius* which first inspired him with a burning desire for an immortal wisdom, and that by what the writer said, not by his manner of saying it.† Cicero is no impersonal writer; we do in fact see the man through all that he writes, sometimes to excess. We are interested even if we do not always admire. His philosophy, eclectic or not, is part of himself; what is noblest in the moral teaching of the schools attracts him by its kinship to his own spirit; he believes that virtue is always expedient, that a man is born not for himself alone but for his fatherland. At times he would accept the ascetic paradoxes of the Stoics, but that his intense humanity comes to the aid of his logic.‡

In what follows I have adhered to the text as closely as possible; save that it seemed well in the case of the large extracts from the Latin to go direct to the originals. It is hoped that these, which include some of the finest passages in our author, will be interesting both in themselves and as essays (they do not pretend to be more) in the art of translating Cicero. To the beginner in Latin prose composition Lord Macaulay's advice may not come amiss : "Soak your mind with Cicero."

N.B.—For the Notes I am alone responsible.

Fettes College, Edinburgh.   W. Y. FAUSSET.

---

* Carm. xlix.
† Conf. iii. 7.
‡ For an impartial review of Cicero's character v. Merivale Hist. III. pp. 2:6-212; also Reid Acad. Introd.; Tyrrell Letters I. introd.

INTRODUCTION.

Vivit vivetque per omnem saeculorum memoriam ; dumque hoc rerum naturae corpus, quod ille paene solus Romanorum animo vidit, ingenio complexus est, eloquentia inluminavit, manebit incolume, comitem aevi sui laudem Ciceronis trahet, citiusque e mundo genus hominum quam Ciceronis gloria e memoria hominum cedet.—*Vell. Paterculus*, ii. 66.

The Roman republic, after subjugating the most powerful kingdoms in all three quarters of the globe, had attained an expansion which contrasted even more strikingly with its original constitution. Such a world-empire, composed of the most diverse countries and peoples, and distracted inwardly by party-strifes, could maintain its unity only by the commanding will of an individual, and from the time of Sulla's dictatorship the internal politics also of Rome tended ever more strongly to monarchy. During this time of transition and violent struggles, in which republican was transformed into monarchical Rome, political interests overpowered all others, and literature, which hitherto had exercised only an indirect action on life, was called upon to take a direct part in the general movement. This, however, holds good only for prose. The storms of the civil war were unfavourable to the growth of poetry, and the few blossoms which it did put forth owed their birth to the private tastes of individuals. On the contrary, all the conditions of the time made for the classical perfection of prose.

Marcus Tullius Cicero by the favour of nature and of circumstances attained supremacy in the domain of literature and became the creator of classical expression in prose. With an unerring tact he knew how to bring into currency just what was suited to the needs and the taste of educated Romans. He stood as a man of, and not above, his own time; he did not trace fresh courses for art or science, but had the capacity of dexterously combining all the several elements of culture belonging to an earlier date, which he had absorbed by diligent study, in such a way that he appeared not as an imitator, but an independent creator. Gifted by nature with an energetic intellect of indefatigable endurance, he had harmoniously trained its several faculties. His lucid understanding, schooled in the reading of the Greek philosophers, gave to his writings that logical order, that clearness and definiteness of thought, by which they so readily adapt themselves to the comprehension of the majority of educated men. To plunge deep into the world of thought, and to bring up new ideas to the light was not within his power. Keen insight enabled him readily to discover others' weak points, and mother wit often served him for a weapon, where logical reasons failed him. Supported by a lively fancy in the rendering and depicting of the occurrences of actual life, he could not rise to poetic creation. An intimate knowledge of the human heart gave him the **means of arousing and allaying its** feelings and passions as every occasion required. **He had** a fine ear for rhythm and sound, but only so far as prose speech required. His intellect no less than his **ear was formed** for symmetry; hence fine proportion is a marked feature alike **in the composition of his works, and in the structure of** the single sentences and periods. **His chief excellence was his fine taste, which led** him to avoid everything that might offend, **whether in form or in matter. He is the** founder and master of the "elegant style," carefully discarding all that **is** antiquated or obsolete, all **that** borders on the vulgar speech **of** the **people.*** **On** this account his writings became the **source of** correct and standard **speech,** a perfect storehouse **of classical prose** diction. He started from the principle that whatever was written should commend itself to all **educated persons.** (*Nobis autem videtur quicquid* **litteris** *mandetur, id commendari omnium* **eruditorum** *lectioni decere.* —*Tusc. ii.* § 8.)

He himself **avows that as an orator he was** the product **not of** the lecture-rooms of **the** rhetoricians, but of the grounds of **the Academy.** (*Fateor me oratorem, si modo sim aut quicunque sim, non* **ex** *rhetorum officinis, sed ex Academiae spatiis exstitisse.*—*Orat.* § 12.)

---

* This **is not to say** that his language, above all in the Letters, **is never colloquial: and,** it must be added, it has occasional **archaisms, which is natural** enough if we remember his familiarity with the older poets of Rome. The student should read Professor Tyrrell's "Correspondence **of Cic.,**" vol. i., introd. ii. § 2 " On the style of the Letters."

Copious expression (*copia*) is a characteristic property of his style, and Caesar too placed his chief merit in this.

Cicero himself in his *Brutus* (§ 253) quotes the following passage in Caesar's treatise *de analogia*: "Some men by study and practice have attained to an admirable power of expressing their thoughts, and we must surely be of opinion that you, who may almost be called the originator and inventor of this fulness of vocabulary, have rendered a signal service to the name and honour of Rome."

Cicero indeed disclaims this praise as proceeding less from conviction than from Caesar's goodwill (*Brutus* 255), but he was fully conscious of his own achievement.

His relation to the Greek masters of eloquence is that of art to nature. What with them is evidence of inborn genius is in him a product of artistic calculation, based upon careful study. He selects from each of his models what is most excellent, and recasts into a single whole. Quintilian has correctly recognised this imitative talent of Cicero.

"He knew," says he (x. i. 108), "that he had wholly devoted himself to the imitation of the Greeks, to uniting the force of Demosthenes, the copiousness of Plato, and the charm of Isocrates; and not only has he made what is best in each of these great men his own; but with the happy fertility of an immortal genius has developed from himself most, or rather all, excellences."

But it is not by formal perfection alone that his writings exert a spell, which is felt even more strongly by posterity than it was by his contemporaries; it is also by the healthy sentiment and the moral earnestness which those writings breathe. Cicero, it may be said, almost belied the Roman character in his tenderness of heart, in the winning humanity of his disposition, in the liberality of his judgment, in reverence for the moral good and dread of wrong, qualities which are the more highly to be prized as he had to combat the temptations of the universal decay of morals. In view of such virtues we readily pardon him the foibles of ambition and vanity which he never once was at the pains to dissemble. The very virtues which made him the great writer whose influence on the moral training of all times has been so beneficent, withheld him as a statesman from achieving the *rôle* to which he believed himself called. He would have had to be more of a Roman, to transport himself beyond all moral considerations, and make himself master of the helm of state, either with the energy of a Caesar or the subtlety of an Octavian.

It argues in him an estimable faith in human goodness, but political shortsightedness and a failure to appreciate the conditions of the time, if by reference to moral duties towards the state and one's fellow-citizens he trusted to be able to allay passions, to recall ambition within the bounds of moderation, and by mediating between parties to save the commonwealth.

He himself confesses that he was early inspired with the wish to play a prominent part. Even as a boy, so he writes to his brother Quintus (*ad Q. fr. iii.* 5), he had chosen for his motto that verse of Homer (*Il*. iv., 208): "Aye to the foremost and excel one's fellows." His brilliant early successes in the forum, his attainment, as a *novus homo*, of the highest offices of state must have fostered this ambition.

At length the fortunate discovery of the Catilinarian conspiracy, and the honours in consequence bestowed on him by the senate, enhanced to the utmost his idea of his statesmanlike capacities. Even in his old age, when the illusion must long since have vanished, in his treatise on moral obligations (*De off*. i. § 77), he presents himself with great self-complacency as the saviour of the state. In his shortsightedness he overlooked the fact that the conspiracy of Catilina was only a symptom of the sickness of the whole body politic, that with its removal the malady had not been cured, but that the dissolution of the body had only been put off for a time. With a signal infatuation he regarded the aristocracy and the senate, out of whose midst the chief conspirators had proceeded, as the state's only anchor of safety, and accordingly followed Pompeius as a loyal adherent, as long as he appeared as the champion of their interest. Undeceived too late, he lost his equilibrium altogether, and his conduct thenceforth was guided no longer by political principles, but by momentary considerations. He retired as soon as possible into private life, despairing of the salvation of the commonwealth, until Caesar's death gave him new hope, and pursuing Antonius as the Philip who alone threatened liberty, he expiated this last infatuation by a violent death.

If Cicero as a writer, thanks to his happy **endowment of mind** and true appreciation of the needs of the time, attained the highest success, for the statesman in a time of revolution and disintegration an abstract ideal of politics could not suffice, unless at least good intention were upheld by a powerful and energetic nature, which would recoil before no difficulty nor from the use of any means. No wonder that his reputation and his talent were in many ways abused by craftier souls: but not even his enemies have been able in any convincing degree to throw suspicion on his moral character. Quintilian (xii. 1) has strikingly deduced from the principle which Cicero too maintained, that only **a** good man could become a good orator, the defence of the two greatest orators of antiquity, Demosthenes and Cicero, against the accusations of their adversaries. "To me," says he, "**it** seems that neither Demosthenes deserves so severe a **verdict** upon his character that I should believe all that his enemies have brought together against him, when I read those most admirable political counsels **of** his, and the story of his death; nor can I see that M. Tullius was **ever untrue** to the purpose **of** a patriotic citizen.

"Witness his famous discharge of the consulship, his absolutely unimpeachable provincial administration, his refusal to enter the college of the *vigintiviri*.* And in those most frightful

---

* A commission of twenty, appointed to execute the agrarian **law** of Caesar's consulship (B.C. 59), providing for the veterans of Pompeius, and **other** needy citizens, by allotments of Campanian land.

civil wars, which fell in his lifetime, neither hope nor fear could dissuade him from attaching himself always to the best party, in other words to the commonwealth. Some think that he failed in courage. He himself gave the best answer to this charge, when he said that he was a coward when dangers were to be apprehended, not when they were to be met.* He proved it too by his death, which he met with signal courage. If these great men fell short of the very highest degree of virtue, we can reply to those who thereupon ask whether they were really orators, with the same answer which would have been given by the Stoics to the question whether Zeno, Cleanthes, and Chrysippus were really wise: That they were great men and worthy of high honours, but withal had not attained to the very highest that human nature can achieve. So too Pythagoras wished that he might not, like his predecessors, be styled a wise man, but one who strove after wisdom."

If finally Cicero's chief rival in antiquity, Asinius Pollio, says of him, " Whereas absolute virtue is the attainment of no mortal, a man must be judged according to the prevalent bent of his life and intellect" (*quando mortalium nulli virtus perfecta contigit, qua maior pars vitae atque ingenii stetit, ea iudicandum de homine est.—Asin. Pollio apud Sen. Suas.* vi.), the severe verdict which Drumann and Mommsen have pronounced upon him, should be reduced to

---

* Non se timidum in suscipiendis sed in providendis periculis.

the milder judgment to be found in the apostrophe which Herder (*Id.* xiv. 5) addresses to him :—

"Rest softly, laborious and much-tried soul, father of the fatherland of all Latin schools in Europe! Whatever thy weaknesses, in life thou hast sufficiently atoned for them: now that thou art dead, tis ours to enjoy the fruits of thy learned, gracious, right-minded, and high-souled intellect, and from thy writings and letters to learn, where we cannot venerate thee, at least to value thee with gratitude and love."

CONTENTS.

	PAGES
INTRODUCTION	...v-xiii
Chapter I.—BIRTH OF CICERO (B.C. 106)—EDUCATION—PUBLIC CAREER TO THE END OF HIS CONSULSHIP (B.C. 63)... ...	1-72
,, II.—FAILURE OF CICERO'S POLITICAL EFFORTS—EXILE AND RETURN UNDER THE TRIUMVIRATE — GOVERNMENT OF CILICIA—CIVIL WAR—SUBMISSION TO CAESAR—LAST STRUGGLE IN THE OPTIMATE CAUSE AGAINST ANTONIUS—DEATH (B.C. 43)	73-147
,, III.—ANCIENT OPINIONS OF CICERO AND HIS ORATORY—HIS WIT—CONTEMPORARY ORATORS—HIS LETTERS ...	148-172
,, IV.—CICERO'S RHETORICAL TREATISES	173-189
,, V.—CICERO'S PHILOSOPHICAL WORKS—MISCELLANEOUS WORK IN PROSE AND VERSE	190-237

ABBREVIATION.

Momms. abr. = Mommsen's History abridged for Schools (Bentley).

MARCUS TULLIUS CICERO.

CHAPTER I.

Birth of Cicero (B.C. 106)—*Education—Public Career, to the End of his Consulship* (B.C. 63).

Birth of Cicero, 3rd January, U.C. 648, **B.C. 106**.

MARCUS TULLIUS CICERO, son of Marcus Tullius and Helvia, was born on January 3rd, U.C. 648, B.C. 106, on his ancestral estate in **the** neighbourhood of the Latin municipium of Arpinum. In later life he never lost his affection for his birthplace. In the second book of the *De Legibus* he transfers the conversation thither, and says to Atticus, "This is my favourite place of sojourn when I wish to give myself up to meditation, or to reading and writing. . . . It **has a** special attractiveness for me as my home, and indeed it **is** said that the wisest of men renounced immortality to see Ithaca once again" (*de legg.* ii. §§ 1-3).

His family, which was of equestrian standing, was as he himself mentions, of very ancient descent, "*orti stirpe antiquissima sumus*" (*de legg.*, *l.c.*). No member of his family before him had been invested with the highest offices of state.

His grandfather, Marcus Tullius, was a plain man, highly esteemed, who lived to see the birth of his famous grandson.

His father, Marcus Tullius, a man of culture, as Cicero himself pourtrays him (*de oratore*, ii. 1), and of respectable connexions, who had held aloof from public offices, went to Rome to procure a better education for his two sons, Marcus and Quintus.

The famous orator Licinius Crassus specially interested himself in the youths, and recommended them to the best teachers of Greek (*de orat.*, ii. 2). Cicero gratefully recognizes the influence which, from his youth until full manhood, the poet Archias had exerted by manifold suggestions on his studies and training (*pro Arch.*, l.). In preparation for his future calling he diligently frequented the forum, and listened to the greatest orators of the day, Lucius

Crassus, **Marcus Antonius,** Sulpicius, **Cotta,** and others.

<small>Assumes toga virilis, U.C. 664, B.C. 90.</small> After assuming the *toga virilis* U.C. 664, B.C. 90, he devoted himself with the greatest zeal to rhetorical study and practice. The old **Mucius** Scaevola the augur, and after his death his namesake the pontiff, the two most notable jurists of their time, initiated him **in the study** of the civil law and in political knowledge. His studies suffered a short interruption by the Marsian War, U.C. 665, B.C. 89, in which he served under Pompeius Strabo. He resumed them on his return. He was first introduced **to** Greek philosophy by the Epicurean Phaedrus (*ad Fam.*, xiii. 1). When, however, in the Mithridatic War, Philo of Larissa, the head of the Academy, fled from Athens to Rome, U.C. 666, B.C. 88, he devoted himself entirely to him, possessed, **as** he says, by **a** wonderful passion for philosophy (*Brut.* 306).

In the same year he was also a diligent pupil **of** the Rhodian rhetorician **Molo, whose** teaching he also enjoyed when he **came again to Rome at the** time of his public appearance as envoy of the Rhodians. During the civic troubles U.C. 666-670, B.C. 88-84, he spent, as he himself mentions (*Brut.*, 308), day and night in the thorough study of the various sciences. He had taken the Stoic Dionysius into his house, and under his guidance he practised himself especially in dialectic, " the quintessence of eloquence " (*quae quasi constricta et adstricta eloquentia putanda est. Brut.*, 309.) With all this he did not omit oral rhetorical practice, alike in the Latin, and also indeed, more frequently, in the Greek language. After the dictator Sulla had restored tranquillity, he commenced his practical career in the forum, well prepared, and not, like the majority, there first beginning to learn his craft (*Brut.*, 311).

At first he appeared in civil actions. One of his earliest speeches is that on behalf of Quinctius, which he delivered in his twenty-sixth year, U.C. 673, B.C. 81 (*Gell.*, xv. 28)

Oratio pro P. Quinctio, U.C. 673, B.C. 81

C. Quinctius, the brother of P. Quinctius, had entered into partnership in a trading concern in Gaul with Sextus Naevius, an auctioneer, notorious for his glib tongue. Naevius, a cunning fellow, had taken particularly good care of his own interest, and when, on the death of C. Quinctius, his brother Publius became partner in the business as his heir, Naevius, who had married a relative of Quinctius, contrived so to manage matters that he was able to lay claim to the whole of Quinctius' means. In the action which was instituted on this account, Naevius, being in favour with persons of good position, succeeded in arranging things so that Quinctius could not appear at the stated time, and the Praetor accordingly adjudicated his possessions to the plaintiff. Against this Quinctius entered protest. The parties were summoned before the judge C. Aquilius. Cicero appeared as Quinctius' advocate, Hortensius, against whom Cicero on this occasion measured himself for the first time, for Naevius.

In the exordium of his speech, Cicero sets forth the difficulties which encountered him in the prosecution of his client's cause. Naevius had on his side the favour of the praetor and the signal oratorical power of his advocate Hortensius; whereas he himself was a novice at the bar, and his client Quinctius a man of no mark, without means or friends. A further disadvantage was that M. Junius, who had originally undertaken the cause of Quinctius, having been called away on public business, he had received the brief so late that no time had been left him for preparation. Still he trusted in the fairness of the judge, who would regard truth rather than words, especially under the unfairness of the arrangement by which he was to speak first, to be followed by Hortensius, the more experienced orator. The exordium concludes thus: "Seeing then that P. Quinctius, confronted and discouraged by so many grave difficulties, has taken refuge in your honour, your love of truth, your compassion; seeing that hitherto the violence of opponents has suffered him to find no such thing as even-handed justice, the opportunity of pleading on equal terms, an impartial tribunal; seeing that on every hand, so far has injustice gone, he has met with hostility and **hindrance**: he entreats and adjures you, C. Aquilius, and you, assessors of the court, in this place at last to enable that equity which outrages at every turn have assaulted and overthrown to assert and establish itself." (*Quinct.*, § 10.)

Cicero proceeds to set forth the case in detail, lays bare the trickery and wiles of Naevius and his tools, and shows how by their cunning it had been rendered physically impossible for Quinctius to appear at the stated time. The speech thus concludes:

"If now Naevius is to have the power to do all that he will; if he is also sure to have the will to do what law forbids; what is there left for Quinctius? What God is he to invoke, what human help to entreat? . . . It is grievous to be ousted from all one's possessions; more grievous still to be ousted by injustice. It is a bitter thing to be swindled by anyone; bitterer still by a kinsman. It is a misfortune to lose one's property; a still graver to lose one's honour too. It is death when the knife is put to one's throat by a worthy and respectable man, but worse than death when this is done by one who has plied his voice for hire as a common crier. It is ignominious to succumb to an equal or a superior; still more to one far our inferior. It is a sad thing to fall with all one's **goods and chattels into** the hands of a stranger; still more into those of a foe.

"It is a formidable matter to have to plead at all with one's civil status at stake: more fearful still **to have to** plead **first.** Quinctius has looked **in** every direction for help, has tried every resource. He has not only failed to find a praetor from whom to obtain justice, or even to claim it with such a form of action as he wished; but even the friends of Naevius have refused him, at whose feet he has often and long prostrated himself, adjuring them by the immortal Gods either to proceed against him in honourable litigation, or while inflicting wrong to spare his good name.

"At length he brought himself to meet his overbearing adversary face to face. Weeping, he seized the hand of Naevius, that hand so well-practised in the proscription of kinsmen's property, he adjured him by his departed brother's ashes, by the name of kinsman, by Naevius' wife and children, to whom none stands nearer than Quinctius, that he would at length admit some pity to **his mind**, that he would respect, if not his kinship, at **least** his age, that **he** would respect, **if not** the man before him, at any rate humanity, that he would make with him any compromise whatever that was not intolerable, before **his** good name was lost.

"Rejected by Naevius, receiving no aid from the friends of Naevius, intimidated and hunted from every tribunal, beside you, Aquilius, he has none to whom **to turn.** . . .

"This only request he makes of you, that it may **be** permitted him to carry back with him the character and the reputation which, now approaching the end of his life's race, he has brought with him before your judgment seat; that a man whose conscientiousness has never yet been questioned, may not in his sixtieth year be branded with shame, ignominy, and degradation; that Naevius may not unblushingly array himself in his property as in the spoils of a foe; that, thanks to your help, he may have the good name which has followed him through life to attend him to the grave."

Nothing is known of the result of the speech.

In the following year, U.C. 674, B.C. 80, Cicero appeared in a criminal trial for the first time as the defender of Sextus Roscius of Ameria (*oratio pro S. Roscio Amerino*). This, the first public case (*causa publica*) which Cicero conducted, was so brilliantly successful that, as he himself says (*Brutus*, 312), thenceforth there was no hesitation about confiding any case whatever to him. By his fearless undertaking and successful conduct of the defence, says Plutarch (*vit. Cic.*, 3), he attracted universal admiration. The elder S. Roscius, a rich landowner of Ameria in Umbria, had been assassinated at Rome. Immediately after this event, two relatives who had been at enmity with him, T. Roscius Magnus and T. Roscius Capito, put themselves in communication with Chrysogonus, the freedman and favourite of Sulla, who contrived means for them to share between them the possessions of the murdered man, and to drive the son and heir Sextus, Roscius, destitute out of his father's

U.C. 674, B.C. 80. Oratio pro S. Roscio Amerino.

house. So long, however, as the latter lived they did not consider themselves safe in the possession of the stolen property. Failing in a secret attempt on his life, they suborned one Erucius to bring against him a charge of parricide.

He had, so the accusation ran, perpetrated the **crime,** because his father, with whom he had been at variance, had relegated him to a remote estate, and finally threatened to disinherit him.

The undertaking of the case was not without danger for the orator, because the attack on Chrysogonus might be regarded as indirectly an attack on Sulla himself.

Cicero in fact guards against this **by** saying (§ 22): "I am well aware that Sulla had no knowledge of all this. . . . Sulla the Fortunate though he be, as indeed he is, nevertheless no one can be *so* fortunate as to possess a great establishment without having in it a single unprincipled servant or freedman." What Ciero states, however, in his exordium **as** the reason why he in particular, young and undistinguished, had undertaken the defence **of a** man universally believed to be innocent, throws so vivid a light on the pressure which the dictator then exercised that we must indeed recognise the courage of the speaker. These are his words: "You wonder, I suppose, judges, what can be the reason, that while so many distinguished speakers and noble men keep their seats, I of all men have risen to speak, I, who neither in age, nor in talent, nor in influence can compare with those who are seated here. All whom you see present before you at this trial are agreed that the wrong wrought by an unprecedented crime ought to be repelled; yet owing to the difficulties of the times they do not venture themselves to repel it. The result is that they are present because they obey the call of duty; they hold their peace from fear of danger. What then? Am I the boldest among them all? By no means. Or am I so much more devoted to duty than the rest? No, I am not so desirous of credit on this score, either as to be ready to take it at the expense of other people. What circumstance then has moved me beyond other people to undertake the cause of

Roscius? I have undertaken it, because if any of those whom you see here present, men of the highest moral weight and dignity, had touched in a single sentence on the present political position (and in the present case such reference cannot be avoided), more would have been construed into his speech than was really to be found there; if I on the contrary utter without reserve all that there is to be uttered, my words will not strike upon the public nor spread abroad with anything like the same effect: then further, whereas no utterance of theirs, from their rank and standing, can pass unnoticed, nor from their age and experience, can it be excused on the plea of thoughtlessness, if I speak somewhat freely, it may be overlooked on the ground that I have not yet entered the service of the state, or pardon may be granted to my youth; though now the idea of pardon has vanished as completely from our state as the habit of fair inquiry."*

The masterly defence is directed to prove that

---

* Rosc. Amer., §§ 1-3.

Roscius had neither motive for so horrible **a crime**, nor the capacity for it, while his adversaries might well be supposed capable of such an action; to them alone had the murdered man's death brought any advantage; their earlier life and their **bent** of mind might well accredit such a charge against them; in fact all the circumstances of the **deed** spoke to their guilt. The result was the acquittal **of** Roscius. The subject afforded ample opportunity for the display of the rhetorical art in emphatic declamation, and the young orator well understood how to improve it. One passage in particular, which treats of the punishment of parricide (c. 25), was received with the warmest applause, **as** Cicero himself avows (*Orat.*, 107). It runs **thus** :* " Solon, the Athenian legislator, provided no punishment for parricide because he deemed it impossible. How much wiser were our ancestors! **For,** recognising **that** there is nothing too hallowed **to** be violated some day by

---

* Rosc. Amer. §§ 70-72.

desperate wickedness, they devised a special punishment for parricides, so that those whom nature herself could not keep within the bounds of duty, might be deterred from wickedness by the severity of the punishment. They ordained that parricides should be sewn up alive in **a** leathern sack and flung into the river. What rare wisdom appears here, judges! Is not their purpose manifest, to sever and remove such a one from contact with everything created, debarring him at one blow from sky, sun, water, and earth, so that the man who had slain him to whom he owed his life should have part no more in any of those elements whereof all life consists? They would not expose their bodies to the wild beasts, lest the very **beasts** should be made more bestial by contact with such a monster; would not cast them naked as they were into the river, lest **when they were washed** down into the sea their presence should pollute the one element which (as men believe) can purify all else that has contracted **a** taint; in fact, they would allow them no share whatever in anything, **however common and** widely diffused. For what is so much the common property of all as air for the living, earth for the dead, the sea for the wave-tossed, the shore for the stranded? Living,—while they can live—they breathe not the air of heaven; dying, their bones touch not the earth; tossed amid the waves, they are not washed by them; stranded at last, not even upon the rocks do they find a resting-place in death." Cicero very justly criticises himself (*Orator*, 107): "All this is in the style of a young man, who has attained praise not for mature performance, but for the hope and promise of such."

U.C. 675, B.C. 79.
Visits Athens and Asia.

In the following year, not so much from fear of the displeasure of Sulla at his independent conduct as from consideration for his impaired health, Cicero was induced to leave Rome for a time.

His delicate bodily constitution, as he tells us (*Brut.*, 313), had been affected by severe study and great exertion of his lungs in speaking, so that his friends and the physicians advised him to relinquish his occupation as an advocate altogether. He would, however, have defied any danger rather than renounce the fame which he hoped to win from oratory.

Eventually he resolved upon a journey to Athens and Asia, which might be serviceable not only for the restoration of his health, but for his technical training also.

At Athens he renewed his acquaintance with T. Pomponius Atticus, and was a hearer of Antiochus of Ascalon, "the most famous and the ablest philosopher of the old Academy." At the same time he practised himself diligently in oratory under the guidance of Demetrius Syrus. After a six-months' sojourn he left Athens and travelled through the Roman province of Asia, everywhere resorting to the most famous rhetoricians, such as Menippus of Stratonice, who was then considered the greatest of his profession in Asia; Dionysius of Magnesia, Aeschylus of Cnidus, Xenocles of Adramyttium. In Rhodes he again met Molo, whose instruction he had already enjoyed at Rome. "His greatest trouble with me was to restrain the exuberance of a juvenile imagination, always ready to overflow its banks, within its due and proper channel" (*Brut.* 316*.)

Here he made the acquaintance of the Stoic Posidonius.

<small>U.C. 677, B.C. 77.
Returns to Rome.</small>
After two years he returned to Rome, U.C. 677, B.C. 77, not only, as he says, better trained, but almost another man (*non modo exercitatior, sed prope mutatus, Brut., l.c.*). His health was re-established and his oratory had gained in manly repose.

He now devoted himself with fresh zeal to public pursuits, and conducted, as he himself tells us, several actions which aroused public interest. (*Brut.*, 318.) The result was that in the year U.C. 678, B.C. 76, he was unanimously elected
<small>U.C. 678, B.C. 76.
Appointed Quaestor.</small>
quaestor. In the following year he received the administration of the province of Lilybaeum in Sicily, and not only earned the confidence and esteem of the inhabitants,

---

* So translated Middleton, Life of Cic., **sect. i.**

but established a special claim upon the gratitude of Rome, by sending thither ample convoys of corn during a severe scarcity. His vanity made him regard himself already as the object of general admiration, of whom all Rome was speaking, until, as he himself tells us with a good deal of humour (*pro Planc.*, 64), he was bitterly undeceived on his return: "I then believed that people at Rome were talking of nothing but my quaestorship. In the greatest scarcity I had dispatched thither a very large quantity of corn, had shown myself friendly to the financiers, just to the merchants, liberal to the revenue-farmers, disinterested towards the allies, to all men most exact in the discharge of every duty; many unprecedented marks of honour had been devised for me by the Sicilians. Accordingly I started from my province in the expectation that the people of Rome would go out of their way to bestow every possible favour on me. But when the course of my journey from the province brought me to Puteoli, then, just at the time (as chance had it) when the neighbourhood is crowded with fashionable visitors, I thought I should have sunk to the earth, when I was asked by someone when I had left Rome, and what was the news there. When I replied to him that I was on my way back from the province, 'To be sure!' said he, 'from Africa, I suppose?' 'No,' I said, superciliously (I was getting angry), 'no, from Sicily!' Hereupon someone else put in his word, with an air of superior information, 'What, don't you know that he has been quaestor at Syracuse?' To cut my story short, I forgot my vexation, and made show as if I were one of the visitors. Yet I am not sure but that this incident did me more service than if at the time everyone had welcomed me with congratulations. For ever since I observed that the Roman people have rather heavy ears, but keen and sharp eyes, I have ceased to think what men would hear about me, but have taken good care that they should see me daily in proper person. I have lived in public view, have worn the pavement of the forum; neither my hall-porter nor the claims of sleep have excluded any from an interview with me."

Of the many forensic speeches which Cicero, according to his own statement (*Brut.*, 319), delivered during the next five years, only one, that for a certain M. Tullius (*oratio pro M. Tullio*), has been preserved, and this in a very fragmentary condition. It was delivered in the year U.C. 682 or 683, B.C. 72 or 71, in an action against one P. Fabius, a Sullan veteran, who had pulled down a country house belonging to Tullius.

U.C. 684, B.C. 70.
Elected Curule Aedile.
Prosecution of Verres
(Divin. in Caecilium:
Verrine Orations).

In the year U.C. 684, B.C. 70 Cicero was unanimously elected curule aedile in spite of various endeavours on the part of his opponents to prevent his election. While still a candidate for this office, he had received from the Sicilians the honourable commission of prosecuting for extortion Caius Verres, who as praetor had for three years plundered and oppressed Sicily in the most shameful way, but was countenanced by men of the highest consideration, Hortensius among them. Besides Cicero, Q. Caecilius Niger, formerly quaestor to Verres, came forward as prosecutor, suborned by Verres himself, in order to prevent the prosecution being undertaken by Cicero. **Manius** Glabrio, the praetor, and his assessors* had to make the choice between Cicero and Caecilius.

In the speech against Caecilius (*Divinatio in Caecilium*) Cicero calls upon the judges to pronounce for him. He first sets forth what has induced him, who heretofore had undertaken defences only, and never a prosecution, to appear as accuser against Verres. It had been done at the suggestion and request of the Sicilians themselves, who ever since his quaestorship had had special confidence in him, and he was discharging an obligation, for at parting he had given them a promise always to maintain their interests. It was, however, no longer a question of their interests, but of their very existence, and the welfare of the whole province.

There were no gods left in their cities to give them sanctuary, for Verres had stolen all the statues

---

* A *consilium* of unsworn *iudices* acted in the process of *divinatio*.

of the gods from their most venerable **temples.**
Whatever wantonness, inhumanity, avarice, arrogance could wreak of outrage, punishment, robberies, and insults, they had experienced personally during his three years' administration.

He had been unable therefore **to** reject their prayers, and his accusation of an individual was in defence of many men, many towns, a whole province.

Even **were** this not so, mere regard for the state required him to consign to punishment the man whose robberies and deeds of shame were related not in Sicily only, but in Achaia, Asia, Pamphylia, ay, in Rome itself. Caecilius was put up as prosecutor, only to bring about the acquittal of Verres.

He was a secret confederate of the latter, and a partner in his crimes. At the same time he lacked the capacity and oratorical training needed if he was to appear with any prospect of success in a case, which attracted the attention of the whole people, against antagonists like Hortensius. If Caecilius alleged that he himself **had** suffered injustice **at the hands** of Verres, this was only a pretence ; for **it was** well known that after the ostensible injury he had lived on the friendliest terms with him. And even allowing that injustice had been done him by Verres, the present question was of punishing wrongs committed not against him, but against the province. Further, it placed him in a bad light, if he, Verres' quaestor, were to accuse his praetor when, according to time-honoured precedent, a quaestor was bound to regard his praetor as a father.*

The result of the speech was that the judges nominated Cicero as prosecutor. Having collected in Sicily itself the necessary body of evidence in fifty days instead of the stipulated period of 110, he renounced the oratorical triumph of a continuous accusation in order to thwart the designs of Verres for the protracting of the trial, and confined himself to a short introductory speech, the so-called *Actio Prima in Verrem*; after which he brought forward each article in the indictment in succession, the evidence of witnesses being taken and the documents read for

---

* *Div. in Caec.* §§ 58-62.

each singly **as it came up. The** result was that Hortensius, the advocate of Verres, threw up his brief, and the latter, who during the proceedings had already retired from Rome, was sentenced to banishment and confiscation. There was no further pro**cedure;** Cicero, however, worked up his **ample** materials into five speeches, the *Actio Secunda in Verrem*, which he subsequently published. They display masterly perfection alike in the arrangement and handling of the material, and also in the rhetorical and verbal garb, on which account Quintilian, in his treatise on rhetoric, has devoted to them special attention. They afford a gloomy picture of the provincial administration of Rome, and furnish weighty contributions towards the understanding of the political and social circumstances of the day.

In the first speech *(De praetura urbana)*, which may be treated as a kind **of** introduction, the earlier life of Verres, personal and official, is illustrated, especially his conduct in the administration of the urban praetorship.

The second speech *(De praetura Siciliensi)* describes

the behaviour of Verres as praetor in Sicily, and chiefly his unjust and iniquitous ordinances and decrees against private individuals, his venality as a judge, his shameless sale of offices and dignities, his extortions of money under pretext of the erection of statues, his malversations **of state** dues in concert with the *publicani*.

The third speech (*De frumento*) exposes his frauds in the collection of the tithes, in the purchase of corn for his own granary, and in the assessment of the corn to be delivered for the state.*

The fourth speech (*De signis*) describes his passion for works of art, which he gratified by the most barefaced plunder of all treasures, public and private.

In the fifth speech (*De suppliciis*) Cicero shows how

---

* This was the threefold impost on the provinces of Sicily and Asia at this period: (*a*) *decumae* of corn, wine &c., levied on the land for Rome: (*b*) *frumentum in cellam* or *aestimatum*, for the praetor and his "cohort": (*c*) *frumentum emptum*, raised from certain lands (*agri decumani*) as a second tithe, sometimes supplemented by *f. imperatum* (an extraordinary supply), and sent at a certain price to the Roman corn market. These burdens were greatly aggravated by the actions of the *publicani*.

little ground the defenders of Verres **had for ex-**tolling him as a general, who, while the Servile war was raging in Italy, had maintained peace in Sicily. This very war had been turned to account by him for fresh extortions; his marches had been pleasure excursions, his camp the rendezvous of abandoned prostitutes, and the most worthless persons of every kind.

The Sicilian fleet, instead of defending the province against pirates, had served Verres simply as a pretext for extorting yet more money. He had shared with the pirates their booty by a private understanding, whilst he punished with the utmost cruelty innocent sea-captains, pretending that they had betrayed the fleet to them. With similar atrocity he proceeded against Roman citizens who repaired to Sicily for the purpose of trade.

To extort money and possess himself of their cargoes, he flung them into the mines, had them **beaten** with rods, and crucified.

He concludes by urging that such a monster must **be** doomed by the judges to an ending worthy of his life and his actions; for his own part he prays that ever henceforth he may have occasion only to defend the good, never again to accuse the impious.

U.C. 685, B.C. 69, Cicero as aedile gave three shows of games, without, however, courting popularity by any lavish expenditure (*Verr.*, **ii. v.** 36; *De off.*, ii. 59).

U.C. 685, B.C. 69.
Orationes pro M. Fonteio, pro A. Caecina, (?) pro Q. Roscio Comoedo.

To this year belong the speeches for Marcus Fonteius and for Aulus Caecina, of the former of which the beginning is lost, a defence against the charge of extortion committed by the accused as praetor in Gaul, the latter respecting a disputed inheritance. To the same year perhaps belongs the speech for Quintus Roscius the comedian, of which the opening and conclusion are missing.

The matter under dispute was the indemnity paid for a slave of Fannius Chaerea, who had been slain by one Flavius. Chaerea, as plantiff, alleged that Roscius, whose stage-pupil the slave had been, had defrauded him in the partition of this money.

Cicero undertook the defence **of his friend, the** famous comedian, of whom in his speech for Quinctius (§ 78) he had already pronounced that his **merits** as an artist were such that he seemed the only man worthy to appear on the stage, his virtues as a man such that he seemed to be the one man who ought not to be seen there. Here too he seizes the opportunity **to** bestow the highest praise alike on the character and on the art of his friend. Amongst other things he says:

"**As fire** no sooner falls into water, than **it** is quenched and chilled, so should a false accusation, worked up against a man of the purest **and** most irreproachable life, instantly collapse. Roscius defraud his partner indeed? Can such an offence attach to such a man? A man whose integrity, I dare confidently say, transcends even his artistic worth; his honesty, his professional skill; whom the public of Rome rates even higher as a man than as an actor; whose art does the highest honour to our stage, as his singlemindedness might do the highest honour to our Senate-house." (*Q. Rosc. com.*, 17.)

In the year U.C. 687, B.C. 67, Cicero was unanimously elected praetor. In the following year he entered on the urban praetorship, his administration of which was exemplary, and delivered his first political speech before the people (*Oratio pro lege Manilia de imperio Cn. Pompeii*) in support of the proposal of the tribune C. Manilius to commit to Cn. Pompeius with unprecedented powers the conduct of the Mithridatic war, Hortensius and Catulus having spoken against the motion of Manilius.

<small>U.C. 687 B.C. 67
Cicero elected Praetor.</small>

<small>U.C. 688, B.C. 66. Oratio pro lege Manilia de imperio Cn. Pompeii; Oratio pro A. Cluentio.</small>

In the exordium he set forth the grounds on which he had heretofore refrained from speaking on political subjects, and the motive which now impelled him to do so:

"Although I have always found the greatest delight in the contemplation of your thronging assemblies, Quirites, and have felt that here is the most illustrious arena for the statesman, the most dignified for **the** orator; yet I have hitherto been withheld, not by my inclination, but by the plan of life which on entering upon man's estate I proposed to myself, from essaying that avenue to fame which has always been open to the highest excellence alone.

"Hitherto, in consideration of my youth, I have never yet ventured to take my stand on this authoritative spot. Convinced that nothing short of the highest product of intellect perfected by labour ought to be brought to this place, I decided to devote my whole time to the exigencies of my friends.

"There has thus never been a lack here of persons to defend your interests, whilst my conscientious and clean-handed labours of private advocacy have earned their fullest reward in your approving verdict. Yes, having in consequence of the adjournment of the comitia three times over headed the list of praetors elected by the vote of all the centuries, I easily learnt, Quirites, what was your opinion of me, and what you required of others. Possessing that measure **of** consideration which you have awarded me in conferring office upon me, that measure of ability as a pleader, which the well-nigh daily practice of speaking has been **able to confer** on a man of energy in the course of his forensic experience, at any rate I shall now employ what measure I possess of the **former** before you who have invested me with it, and **whatever** results I **can** attain as a speaker I shall exhibit to those first and foremost who have thought fit by their decision to confer on this gift of mine also its reward. And here first I find ground to congratulate myself that, unused as I am to speaking in this place, the subject put before me is one on which no one can fail to find words. I have to speak of the eminent and matchless merits of Cneius Pompeius, and with such a theme the difficulty is rather to find an end than a beginning. In fact I have not so much to seek material as limits for my speech."

After briefly detailing the outbreak and the course of the Mithridatic war down to the date of speaking, the orator pourtrays its difficulty and importance and shows the necessity of bringing it definitely to an end. **Only a** general such as Pompeius can speedily and prosperously terminate it; for he alone possesses all the requisite attainments and qualities of a general, **as the** previous wars carried on by him prove. To the objection of Hortensius that everything ought not to be committed to one man, there was an answer in the recent termination of the war with the pirates by one man, Pompeius. To that of Catulus, that Pompeius should not expose himself **to** this danger, that the whole hope of the Roman people rests upon him, that old Roman precedent and prescription forbid the **committal** of everything to one **man,** the reply is that the state must avail itself of the life and the valour of so distinguished a man, so long as the gods vouchsafe the opportunity, and the men of old too had always acted according to the circumstances of the times; besides, the rare deserts of Pompeius called for an extraordinary requital. In conclusion the orator once more urges the acceptance of the Manilian Rogation, and avows that he urges this, not from regard for Pompeius, but for the highest good of the state.

The speech is distinguished not only by its rhetorical excellence, but also by the delicacy with which the orator, while exalting the deserts of

Pompeius, does justice to the earlier leaders in the struggle, notably to Lucullus, and by the moving pathos with which he incites the people to the most vigorous prosecution of the war.

Amongst other passages is the following (§ 11):

" Your forefathers often waged wars because Roman traders and shippers had been treated with indignity; now, after that so many thousands of Roman citizens have been butchered at one time by a single stroke of the pen, what should your feelings be?

" For contemptuous words addressed to their envoys your fathers decreed the extinction of Corinth, the eye of all Greece; will you let go unavenged the king who has done to death the envoy of the Roman people, a former consul,* with bonds and stripes and every form of torture? They would not brook an interference with the freedom of Roman citizens; will you make light of their murder? They vindicated a verbal outrage on the privilege of an embassy; will you allow the murder, amid the worst torments,

---

* M'. Aquillius.

of an ambassador of the Roman people to go unpunished? See to it that while it was their highest honour to bequeath to you this mighty and glorious empire, it be not your deepest disgrace to prove unable to maintain and defend what you have received."

The speech had the most brilliant success. The Bill was passed, and Pompeius appointed commander.

To the same year, U.C. 688, B.C. 66, belongs the speech *pro Aulo Cluentio Habito*. Cluentius had been accused of poisoning his stepfather Oppianicus.* This speech reveals a tissue of crimes of all sorts, incest, murder, forgeries, and bribery, perpetrated by Sassia, the mother of Cluentius, and her husband Oppianicus. Oppianicus, having been previously accused by Cluentius of attempting to poison him,

---

* Cluentius was indicted under the murder-law of Sulla, *Lex Cornelia de Sicariis et Veneficis*, and it is probable, though not certain, that, besides the charge of poisoning, he had to answer to a charge of having used bribery at the previous trial to procure the condemnation of Oppianicus. Such an act of "judicial murder" was indictable under another clause of the same *lex Cornelia*.

had been condemned, and had escaped the penalty*
by voluntary exile, in which he died. After his death
Cluentius' own mother raised the suspicion that it
was due to poison which Cluentius had caused to be
administered to him. She sought to support it by
the utterances of a slave, who, having been put to the
torture for a theft, was alleged to have confessed to
this matter also.

In the year U.C. 689, B.C. 65, Cicero delivered the two speeches for Cornelius,

U.C. 689, B.C. 65.
Orationes pro C. Cornelio.

who had been accused of treason, in opposition to Catulus and Hortensius. Cicero himself reckoned these among his best speeches, and in his *Orator* (§§ 225, 232), speaking of cadence and rhythm, quotes from them several typical examples.

Quintilian (viii. 3) depicts the ecstasy into which these speeches threw the Roman people. An orator, says he, in order to transport his hearers, must know how to fight with weapons, not only strong but bright;

---

* *Aquae et ignis interdictio.*

as an illustration he **refers to the extraordinary** success which Cicero had in this way attained in the trial of Cornelius. The Roman people had expressed their admiration, not only by cheers but with clapping of hands. "To have elicited such a storm of applause the language must have been elevated, stately, brilliant, impressive. So extraordinary **a** testimony would not have fallen to the lot of the orator had the speech kept in the ordinary track, and been just like all the rest. I believe that the audience lost all consciousness of what they were doing, and uttered their plaudits not consciously or deliberately, but being as it were beside themselves, **and** forgetting where they were, broke out into this violent expression of their delight."

Of these speeches we possess only fragments.

In the following year, U.C. 690, B.C. 64, Cicero stood for the consulship, and, in spite of the manifold intrigues **of his** opponents, succeeded **in** attain**ing** this highest dignity as he had all previous offices

<small>U.C. 690, B.C. 64. Cicero elected Consul.</small>

at the earliest lawful date (*legitimo anno*), though a *novus homo*, by a unanimous vote.

In the first speeches which he delivered as consul, the three speeches on the proposed agrarian law in opposition to Servilius Rullus, he showed what the principles of his consular administration were to be, thus issuing as it were its programme.

U.C. 691, B.C. 63. De lege agraria contra L. Servilium Rullum Orationes iii. Oratio pro C. Rabirio perduellionis reo: Orationes iv. in L. Catilinam: Oratio pro L. Murena.

The tribune Rullus intended to propose an agrarian enactment under which a commission of ten was to be elected with almost unlimited powers, with a view to the purchase and distribution of lands among the people. In the speech which Cicero delivered in the senate upon his entrance into office on the 1st of January, U.C. 691, B.C. 63, is the following passage: "You are gravely mistaken, alike you, Rullus, and some of your colleagues, who have hoped in opposition to a consul, who is in the true not the specious sense a friend of the people, yourselves to pass for such, while you are really ruining the commonwealth. I challenge you, I invite you to a public meeting : I would have the people of Rome for arbitrator between us. Look round as we may to find what is pleasing and acceptable to the people, we shall find nothing so popular as peace, harmony, and quietude. . . . I am steadfastly purposed and resolved to adopt in my consulship what is the only dignified and independent course, namely to entertain no desire for any province, any honour, any distinction, any advantage, in short, anything whatever which a tribune may be able to obstruct . . . I will so act in this office conferred on me by the sovereign people, that I may be able to bridle any resentment of the tribunes against the commonwealth, to scorn any against myself." (§§ 23, 25, 26.) In a longer speech to the people which he afterwards delivered, he first thanks them for his election to the consulate, and repeats what he had already said in the senate, that he should be a consul of popular sympathies. "For I absolutely can take no other course, having been elected consul as I well know, not by the devotion of the powerful, not by the exceptional influence of the few, but by the verdict of the whole Roman people, and that in marked preference to the very noblest competitors; I must needs show myself alike during my term of office, and during my whole future life, a friend of the people. . . . . .

"Yes, I have said in the senate, I mean to be a popular consul. For what is so popular as peace, at which not only sentient creatures, but the very houses and the fields seem to me to express their joy? What so popular as freedom, which, as you see, is coveted and preferred to everything, not only by men, but by the irrational animals? What so popular as quiet, a boon so welcome that you believe, as does every man of spirit, that you are bound to endure the greatest exertions in order to be able some day to live in quiet? . . . How, in short, can I be anything but popular, when I see, Quirites, that all this peace abroad, the special freedom of your own race and name, internal quiet, everything, in a word, which you prize or honour, has been placed in my safe-keeping, as consul, and under my patronage?

"It is not this, Quirites, which should be acceptable

and popular in your eyes—the proposal of a distribution, which may be paraded in fine language, but can actually be carried into effect only by draining the public treasury—these are not what ought to be accounted popular measures, rude interferences with the courts of law, annulments of sentences delivered, the restoration of the condemned: proceedings such as form the closing scenes of ruin in the already doomed fortunes of shattered states. And when men promise lands to the Roman people, but all the time secretly entertain some design different from the mirage of hope with which they would lure you, popular is no name for such as these. For, Quirites, to speak frankly, I cannot blame an agrarian enactment in itself; . . . but when I examine that of Rullus, I find from first to last sections of no other import, aim, or purpose than this—that, under the style and pretence of an agrarian law, ten kings are to be installed as lords over the treasury, over the taxes, over all the provinces, over the whole commonwealth, over the dependent kingdoms, over the free peoples, in short, over the world.

"Of this I assure **you**, Quirites, under this fair-seeming and popular agrarian law, nothing is given to you, a chosen few receive a present of everything; **lands are** dangled before the eyes of the Roman people* while they are being despoiled of their freedom; the purse of individuals is being filled, while that of the public is being drained. Crowning shame **of all**, through the tribunes, whom **our** fathers designed as the prime champions and guards of freedom, kings are being established in our commonwealth." (Cc. 3, 4, 6, §§ 7-16.)

The result of the speech **was** that Rullus did not venture to proceed further with his bill.†

---

* Reading *populo Romano.*

† **Cicero's** chief objection to the bill relates to the excessive powers to be conferred on the *decemviri* who shall execute its provisions: *orbis terrarum gentiumque omnium datur cognitio sine consilio, poena sine provocatione, animadversio sine auxilio.* The optimates had already conceded extraordinary powers to Pompeius, but they **were** loath to make a similar concession to his political rivals, Crassus and Caesar, on whom (with others) the democratic **party, from which this** bill proceeded, was certain to confer **the powers proposed.** *V.* Mommsen, iv. 1, 171; **Mommsen, abr., p. 379;** Boissier, *Cic. et ses amis,* p. 48.

An ancient **estimate of these** speeches **of** Cic. is worth quoting:—"Sed quo te, M. Tulli, piaculo taceam quove maxime

Hereupon the tribunes alleged against Cicero, that his design in opposing the agrarian enactment had **been** merely to advantage the holders of Sulla's assignations (*possessoribus Sullanarum assignationum*). Against this Cicero defends himself in his short third speech to the people.

Another episode in the same struggle to excite the people against the optimates was the accusation of Caius Rabirius. This aged senator was prosecuted **by** the **tribune** Titus Atius Labienus, as the murderer of the turbulent tribune Saturninus, slain thirty-six years before.* Cicero defended him before the people (*Oratio pro C. Rabirio perduellionis reo*), and was able to boast that in exonerating Rabirius from the charge of treason, he had upheld and de-

---

excellentem insigni praedicem? Quo potius quam universi populi illius gentis amplissimo testimonio, e tota vita tua consulatus tantum operibus electis? Te dicente legem agrariam, hoc est alimenta sua, abdicaverunt cives." (Plin. nat. hist., vii. 31, 116.)

At the same time the Servilian rogation was in the main both wise and moderate, and Cicero's opposition does less credit to him as a statesman than as a partisan pleader.

* Mommsen, iii. **215**; Mommsen, abr. 262.

fended against popular ill-will, the authority of the senate which had been pledged to a certain cause forty years before the date of his consulship (*in Pis.* § 4). "You allege," says he, "that L. Saturninus was slain by C. Rabirius; and yet Rabirius, defended exhaustively by Q. Hortensius, and citing the evidence of numerous witnesses, has already disproved the charge. For my part, were the question an open one for me, I would take the responsibility, would acknowledge and avow the charge. Yes, I only wish the circumstances of the case left me free to proclaim that L. Saturninus, enemy of the Roman people, was slain by the hand of C. Rabirius! [Murmurs of dissent.] That outcry does not disturb me one whit, it reassures me; it suggests that there are some ill-informed citizens here, but not many. Never, believe me, would the people of Rome—these silent listeners —have made me consul, had they deemed that I should be disconcerted by your outcry. Ah! how the murmur is abating already! Better save your breath! your voice only betrays your folly, and testifies to your scanty numbers!

"Gladly, I say, **would** I avow, if I could **with truth, or if it** were open to me **to do** so, that Saturninus was slain by the hand of Rabirius ; I should deem it a most glorious deed ; **but as** I cannot do this, I will avow what will redound **to** his praise the less, though **none the less to** the support of the indictment, that Rabirius took **up** arms for the **purpose** of slaying Saturninus." (§18.) "But when **every** eminent man in the state was taking part with the consuls, what **was** the proper course for Rabirius to take ? **was he to** skulk in privacy and retirement ? to screen his cowardice from the light of day behind the walls of his house ? **or** to repair **to** the Capitol, and herd there with your uncle, and the rest who sought in death escape from the disgrace of their life ? **Or** was he **to** enter into partnership with Marius, Scaurus, Catulus, Metellus, Scaevola, and **all** loyal citizens in their perils as much as **in** their deliverance ? " (§21.)

"If we are to condemn Rabirius, **we** must with him condemn also, now that **they are dead, all** these great men, **and** in particular Caius Marius. But, says Labienus, what harm can that do to Marius, who has now lost life and conscious existence? Is that really so? Would Marius have lived a life of toil and danger, had he not **cherished** a hope of renown beyond what the bounds of this present life would admit? I am to believe, forsooth, that, when **in** Italy he routed the innumerable forces of the foe and rescued his country from a state of siege,* he expected all his services to die with himself.

"Not so, Quirites; there is no one who manfully and meritoriously encounters peril on behalf of the commonwealth without being impelled by the hope of reward from posterity.

"Yes, amid the many reasons for thinking that the minds of the good are deathless and divine, this is to my mind the strongest, that every wise and virtuous soul by its presage **of a** hereafter shows **that it** looks for nothing less than immortality.

"So thinking, I call to witness the souls of Marius **and those** other wise men and gallant citizens, who

---

* Sc. by **arresting the** inroad of the Cimbri at Vercellae in the **north** of Italy. *V.* Mr. Heitland's note.

have passed, as I hold, from human life to the dread and hallowed state of the gods, that I deem it my duty to champion their fame, their renown and memory no less than our country's shrines and temples; and had I to take up arms for their honour, I would do so no less resolutely than they did for the common welfare. You know, Quirites, that nature has traced for us a path of life which has its bounds, a path of glory which is boundless." (§ 30.)

The Praetor, Metellus Celer, contrived to prevent a decision by the people, and Labienus allowed the charge to drop.

Unable to accomplish their objects in the senate and the forum, the enemies of the state at last attempted to attain them by a conspiracy of which Lucius Catilina was the head. But their secret machinations equally failed to elude the consul's vigilance. All precautions were taken to obviate the danger, and in the speech which Cicero delivered before the senate in the temple of Jupiter Stator (*oratio I. in L. Catilinam*) the consul addressed himself directly to Catilina, present before him: "How much longer, Catilina, will you abuse our forbearance? How long is your frenzy still to run riot? How far will your unbridled effrontery flaunt itself? **The sentinels at** night upon the Palatine, the piquets throughout the city, the public alarm, the mustering of all loyal men, the meeting of the senate in this spot so strongly defended, the mien and aspect of those before you—are you unmoved **by all this?** Do you not perceive that your designs are exposed? **Can you not** see that, with all here present apprised of it, your conspiracy is held in **a** vice? Your doings **of last** night and the night before, the place you were at, the men you convened, **the resolve** you took—which of us, think you, does **not know** it all? '*O tempora! o mores!*' The senate perceives, the consul sees it; and yet *he* lives! Lives! ay, and enters the senate, shares in public deliberations; marks down and singles out with his **eye each one of** us for massacre. And we—brave spirits!—are **supposed to do** our **duty by** the commonwealth, **if we evade his frenzy** and his weapons. Long ere this, Catilina, you ought to have been haled to execution at the consul's command; and the destruction brought upon yourself which you have so long been plotting against us all." (§§ 1-2.) "You live still, and live, not to renounce but to emphasise your effrontery. I wish, conscript fathers, to be merciful; I wish, amid the great perils of the commonwealth to avoid the appearance of remissness; but I am really beginning to condemn myself **for** apathy and moral cowardice. There is in Italy, in the defiles of Etruria, a camp planted against the Roman people; the number of the enemy is increasing from day to day; the commander of that camp, the chief of those foes we see within our walls, ay, in the senate, daily meditating some deadly blow against the innermost heart of the commonwealth. Should I at this moment, Catilina, order your arrest, your execution, I think I may safely say that all patriots will find fault with my action as tardy, sooner than anyone whatever will find fault with it as cruel. But, though this step should have been taken long ago, there **is a** distinct motive which **induces me for the present to refrain.**

"Then only shall you meet your death, when no one can be found so unprincipled, so abandoned, so like yourself as not to acknowledge the justice of your fate. So long as there is anyone bold enough to defend you, be it but one man, you shall live, but only as you are now living, overawed by my sentries in such numbers and such strength that you cannot stir a step against the state. Many watchful eyes and ears will still as heretofore observe your movements, when you little think it." (§§ 4-6.)

The orator proceeds to point out that it was not at present a question of consigning Catilina to a well-deserved death, but only of his withdrawing himself from the city. If he would only exile himself or betake himself to the camp of Manlius; there the conspiracy stands revealed, the plans of the conspirators are avowed, like the life and aims of Catilina, their originator and head.

His own wish and inclinations were drawing him to the camp of Manlius. Would he but go once and for all! **It was** true his country might ask of the speaker: "What are you about, M. Tullius? Are you going to allow the man to go forth, whom you have ascertained to be a public enemy, in whom you descry the hostile leader that is to be, who you can see is awaited in the camp of the foe as its commander, the instigator of crime, the arch-conspirator, who has rallied slaves and renegade citizens to the standard of rebellion—letting it appear that far from relieving the city of his presence you have let him loose upon it?

"Will you not order him to be thrown into prison, carried off to execution, despatched without mercy? What in the world prevents you? Ancestral custom? Why, again and again in this commonwealth of ours even private persons have inflicted on mischievous citizens the death-penalty.

"The laws that have been passed touching the punishment of Roman citizens? Never yet in this city have those who revolted against the republic retained the rights of citizens. Or do you dread the odium of posterity? On the contrary you are making a noble return to the Roman people, which thus early has exalted you, a man known only on your own merits, with no ancestors to recommend you, through all the grades of office to the highest magistracy, if because of the fear of odium or any peril you disregard the safety of your countrymen. But if there is any fear of odium, should that which attaches to stern and rigorous action be more dreaded than that due to apathy and moral cowardice?

"When Italy is wasted with war, its cities harried, its houses ablaze, will you not then, think you, be scorched by the flame of odium?" (§§ 27-29.) "Here is my brief answer to these sacred pleadings of my country, and to the reflections of those who share the feeling which I have described. If, conscript fathers, I deemed that the best course to take was to inflict on Catilina the punishment of death, I would not have given that gladiator an hour's lease of life. For if eminent men and distinguished citizens by shedding the blood of Saturninus, the Gracchi, Flaccus and many before, far from sullying their good name, ennobled it, certainly I had no reason to dread that by taking the life of this assassin of his brother-citizens any odium would accrue to me in the estimation of posterity. But, were it never so imminent, yet it has ever been my idea to account odium incurred through well-doing no odium, but glory.

"Some, however, there are in the senatorial order, who either fail to see what is imminent, or seeing, will not own to it; and they by their smooth words have fostered Catilina's hopes, and by their incredulity have strengthened the infant conspiracy; and under their guidance many persons, ill-affected or ill-informed, would have pronounced my conduct cruel and despotic, if I had proceeded to extremities against this man. As it is, I feel sure that if he arrives, as he purposes, at the camp of Manlius there will be no one so foolish as not to see that a conspiracy has been formed, so unprincipled as not to acknowledge the fact.

"But by his single death, I am aware, the malady of the country can be arrested for a while, not permanently subdued. But if he makes off, and leads out his followers with him, and gathers there at one centre the rest of his shipwrecked crew, then not only

will this full-grown malady of the state be eradicated,
but the seed and germ of all our evils too. We have
in fact, conscript fathers, for this long time past been
living amid the perils and plots of conspiracy; but
for some reason the manifold crime, the long-standing
frenzy, and daring wickedness has come to ripeness,
and burst in storm upon the time of my consulate.
If out of all that bandit crew this offender only is
removed, we shall perhaps for some short time feel
relieved of our anxiety and apprehension, but the
danger will lurk below, deeply lodged in the veins and
vitals of the state. Just as frequently men suffering
from grave illness, tossing with fever-heat, if they
drink cold water, seem at first to be relieved, but
afterwards are much more sorely and grievously
prostrated, so our country's present disease alleviated
by his punishment will only grow in malignity if the
rest are left alive. Let the traitors retire then, sunder
themselves from the loyal, troop to one spot; let them
at length, as I have already said repeatedly, put the
city-wall between themselves and us; let them
cease to lay ambush for the consul in his own

house,* to beset the tribunal of the city praetor, to beleaguer the senate-house sword in hand, to store up fireballs and brands for burning the city; let each man have his political sentiments written on his brow.

"I promise you this, conscript fathers, that such vigilance shall be found in us the consuls, such moral authority in yourselves, such manliness in the Roman knights, such unanimity among all loyal citizens, that with the departure of Catilina you shall see all laid bare, brought to light, crushed and condignly punished.

"With these prophetic words of mine, Catilina, go your way; to your country's full deliverance, to your own bane and ruin, to the destruction of those your partners in parricidal murder and crime of every sort, go on to your unnatural and impious campaign. Thou, Jupiter, whose sanctuary Romulus established here under the same auspices as the city itself, thou

---

* *V.* Mommsen iv. I. pp. 174, 175; Mommsen abr. p. 389: probably the attempt was made on the night of Nov. 6; and the first speech delivered on Nov. 7. But *v.* Upcott Cic. in Catil. p 12, for a different view. Sall. Catil. chs. 27, 28, may be compared.

whom we truly name the Stablisher of this city and empire, wilt ward off him and his fellows from thine altars and all other shrines, from the city's dwellings and its walls, from the lives and possessions of its citizens, and on these men, enemies of the good, foes of their fatherland, robbers of Italy, leagued together by a compact and wicked partnership of crime, will visit unending punishment in life and death." (§§ 29-33.)

Catilina replied at first in the tones of humility begging the senate not to give too hasty credence to the accusations of his enemies. But when the senators, interrupting his speech, denounced him as an enemy and a traitor, he furiously broke out into violent execrations, and left the senate with this threat: "Driven to extremities as I am by my foes, I will put out my own fire in general ruin." (*Sall. Cat.* 31.)

The same night, accompanied by a few followers, he quitted Rome for the camp of Manlius, after urging Lentulus, Cethegus, and others whom he left behind, to hurry on their plans, with the promise to appear shortly with a large army before the walls of Rome.

Next day* Cicero delivered in the Forum a speech to the people (*Oratio II. in L. Catilinam*). He congratulates himself and the senate on Catilina's disappearance: "He has gone, departed, escaped, broken loose! No longer within our city's very walls will that portentous monster be plotting those walls' destruction."

Intestine conflict has now been made impossible; **an external** conflict has no danger for the **state**. Against the possible censure of the well-affected, that he had acted too mildly towards Catilina, Cicero defends himself on the ground of necessity, as he had not had properly speaking any matter of fact to exhibit against him, and of the purpose in view, by **the** flight of Catilina to drag **to** daylight the conspiracy still secretly lurking

The opposite objection **of** Catilina's friends **that by** his grievous reproaches he had driven him into exile,

---

* November 8th.

he meets with the consideration that Catilina was not the man to allow himself to be intimidated if he had not felt himself guilty.

Further, not the speaker only, but the whole senate had recognised Catilina's guilt, and he himself had confirmed it, by going not into voluntary exile but to the camp of Manlius, to carry on war against the country and the city. Catilina by his flight had recorded his confession that he was an enemy: but there were still many in Rome and without, who were such no less, though unconfessed; the whole crew of embarrassed debtors, of ambitious malcontents; the veterans, who, having squandered their booty, were now wishing for Sulla's times over again; spendthrifts, adventurers, gamblers, murderers, daredevils of every kind. Such of them as might yet be reformed, he would rather bring back to their senses, and reconcile with their country than punish: those who were past amendment should experience his utmost rigour. The gates of the city still stood open for them. Let them go forth to join Catilina in the camp of Manlius, and there form their commander's bodyguard.

Against such a host victory was fairly assured. For the peace of the city he, the consul, would himself provide with the help of the gods.

The conspirators who remained in the city did not allow themselves to be misled by the retirement of Catilina, but went on with their preparations for the outbreak. Cicero obtained information of everything, but did not venture to intervene without having sure proofs in his hands. These were furnished him by the thoughtlessness of the conspirators themselves. Ambassadors of the Allobroges, present in Rome at the time, betrayed to him the fact that the conspirators had made overtures to them to induce their countrymen to join in the rising. Cicero instructed them to make a show of engaging in the plot, and then, on the night of the 2nd and 3rd December when the ambassadors were leaving with the despatches of Lentulus, accompanied by Volturcius, who bore a letter to Catilina, he had them arrested at the Mulvian bridge. Next day the consul laid the documents before the senate in the temple of Concord, and the arrest of the chief conspirators was decided upon, after they had confessed their guilt in the senate.

The same evening* Cicero appeared before the people, and delivered to them an account of the day's proceedings. (*Oratio III. in L. Catilinam.*) He announced that by the favour of the gods and by his own exertions the state, the lives and fortunes of the citizens, the sovereign seat of the Roman Empire had been delivered.

He recounted how the documents which revealed the conspiracy had come into his hands, how Volturcius and the deputies had given their evidence in the senate, how writings and seals had been acknowledged by the conspirators as their own, and how upon search of Cethegus' house a large quantity of daggers and swords had been discovered.

He proceeds to inform them of the resolutions passed by the senate.

First a vote of thanks, couched in the most honourable terms, had been tendered to the consul,

---

* December 3.

and the loyal services of the two praetors, L. Flaccus and Pomptinius, in the apprehension of the ambassadors, acknowledged with commendation. The conspirators had then been declared to have vacated their offices, and their arrest had been ordered. Finally, the consul had been charged to institute in his own name a thanksgiving (*supplicatio*) to the gods "for his having preserved the city from conflagration, the citizens from massacre, Italy from war"— an honour which from the founding of the city had never before fallen to the lot of any magistrate in the garb of peace. If this thanksgiving, he continues, be compared with others, this difference will be found, that those were ordained for successes, this, for the very salvation of the state. For now that the most dangerous leaders of the conspiracy are in safe keeping, all the hope and the strength of Catilina is gone. Had he remained in the city, his cunning and address would have made it difficult for proof of the conspiracy to reach the consul's hands; it is due to his absence that it has been more thoroughly brought to light, than ever was any act of theft in a private house. Let them learn hence to recognise the providential working of the gods, who had previously given warning in the heavens and on the earth, and had now granted the consul the insight and the resolution to bring about such a result, whilst they had so far bereft the conspirators of their senses, that they disclosed their plans and confided damning evidence to barbarian strangers.

Therefore let the citizens, with their wives and children, joyously celebrate the festival; for reward to himself he would have them accord him not any signal mark of honour, not any memorial for fame —only let them cherish eternally the recollection of this day.

He would endeavour as a private person to guard that which as consul he had achieved, and ever to invest it with fresh splendour.

Two days afterwards, on the fifth of December, the Senate assembled in the temple of Concord, to deliberate on the punishment of the conspirators. Two opinions came up for discussion. D. Junius Silanus, the consul-designate, voted for death : C. Julius Caesar, the consul-designate, opposed the death-penalty, and proposed to confine the offenders for **life separ**ately in specified *municipia*, and to confiscate their goods. Hereupon Cicero delivered his judgment as consul in a longer speech. (*Oratio IV. in L. Catilinam.*) Every eye, he said, was fixed upon him; not only the danger **of** the state, but his own filled them with anxiety.

For him, however, they need take no thought; **if the** consulship were his on condition **of** enduring every possible bitterness, sorrow, and torment, he would endure all not only steadfastly, but gladly, provided that by his sufferings the honour and welfare of senate and people were insured. The fate **of** the prisoners must be decided before nightfall.

Two opinions had found support, those of Silanus and of Caesar. Both, as befitted their dignity and the gravity **of** the circumstances, took **a** highly serious **view of the** question. The one believed that those **who** had endeavoured **to** take the lives of all, to overthrow the Roman state and efface the Roman name, ought not to be allowed for another moment to enjoy the life or breathe the air, which all breathe ; and reminded them that such a punishment had often been brought into requisition against treasonable citizens. The other maintained that death was not ordained by the immortal gods as a punishment for offences, but was either a natural necessity, or a release from troubles and hardships. The wise had therefore never been reluctant, the brave often glad to encounter it.

Imprisonment, lifelong imprisonment, had been devised as the special punishment of infamous crime. Their bonds, so Caesar proposed, were never to be loosed; thus he deprives them of hope, that sole consolation of the wretched. He urged also the confiscation of their property, he left them nothing but their bare lives, for were he to take these, then with a single pang he would release them from many, nay from every, form of punishment in body or soul. For this reason, in order that wicked men might have before them an image of terror in the present life, those of old had induced the belief* that punishments of the kind were ordained in the world below for the impious, because they recognised that without this belief, death in itself had nothing formidable.

If now, continues Cicero, it were his own affair to decide between the two proposals, he would doubtless by following the so-called popular proposal of Caesar run less risk of the attacks of the popular party; but consideration for his own danger must yield to the general good. He therefore supported the punishment proposed by Silanus, which was also really the milder, though at the same time no punishment could be severe enough for the enormity of the offence. Otherwise it was to be feared that in dealing lightly with the offenders they might be dealing cruelly with the country.

---

* Thus in Cluent. § 171, the punishments of Hades are called 'ineptae fabulae': Nat. D. ii. § 5; and so most educated Romans thought; Lucretius finds a real Cerberus and Furies in this life:—

"Metus *in vita* poenarum pro male factis" (iii. 1027). Not so, however, Virgil:—

"Sedet aeternumque sedebit Infelix Theseus" (A. vi. 617).

F

The difficulty raised by some persons as to whether the state were sufficiently prepared to deal with a possible outbreak of disorder was of no moment. Everything was provided for, all the citizens, save only the few friends of the conspirators, were animated by the best of feelings.

"Never," he concludes, "shall I regret my course of action, even if the traitor crew should after all gain the day. Death awaits all, and in life no one has ever yet attained such renown as that with which you have distinguished me by your decrees. . . . So long as you keep my consulate in remembrance I shall deem myself sheltered by the strongest of ramparts. . . . Whatever your decision may be you have a consul who will never hesitate to render obedience to your decrees; one who, while he lives, will ever maintain your decisions and make himself responsible for them."

Cato, plebeian tribune-designate, made the speech which turned the scale. He declared unreservedly that anyone who voted for a lighter punishment than death courted the suspicion of complicity in the conspiracy.

Sentence of death was pronounced upon five conspirators, and soon afterwards carried out without any appeal to the people.* The whole senate and people accompanied the consul to his house, acclaiming him as their preserver and liberator, and the father of his country.

It was indeed a day of honour for the great orator, the zenith of his life's glory, but also the origin of much subsequent misfortune and suffering. He himself, in his poem on his consulate, boasted:

> "Rome by my consulate born anew to weal!"
> "O fortunatam natam me consule Romam!"

Only a few weeks after, when Cicero laid down his office as consul, the tribune Q. Metellus vetoed him from expressing himself in a prolonged speech upon his conduct in office, and only allowed him to take the customary oath.†

---

* *V.* Upcott, Catil. Or., p. 16, on the much-disputed question of the legality of the act.

† Ad fam. v. 2, 7, cum ille mihi nihil nisi ut iurarem permitteret, magna voce iuravi verissimum pulcherrimumque ius iurandum, quod populus item magna voce me vere iurasse iuravit. The oath was "Rem publicam atque hanc urbem mea unius opera esse salvam," in Pis. § 6. So Plut., Cic. 23, who adds that it was οὐ τὸν πάτριον ἀλλ' ἴδιόν τινα καὶ καινὸν ὅρκον; so that in *form* at least it was not the customary oath.

At the time when Cicero was engaged in the detection of the Catilinarian conspiracy he also defended L. Licinius Murena, the consul-designate for the following year, whom Ser. Sulpicius Rufus, the famous jurist, his competitor in the canvass for the consulship, along with M. Percius Cato, the zealous Stoic, tribune-elect of the plebs, and Cn. Postumius had accused of bribery (*Oratio pro L. Murena*).

Little doubt as there could be of the guilt of the accused, under the statutory provisions which had been sharpened by Cicero himself as consul in the enactment of the *Lex Tullia*, he contrived by his clever and witty speech to draw off attention from the main issue and to procure the acquittal of his client. The following passages are significant as indicating the ideas of the time and of Cicero himself: " Cato calls Murena a stage-dancer. That is an epithet, if it be truly applied, of passionate accusation ; if falsely, of scurrilous libel. A man of your moral weight, Cato, ought not to catch up an abusive epithet from the street-corners, and inconsiderately call the consul of the Roman people a dancer, but must first reflect what further blemishes must adhere to one against whom such an imputation can with truth be made. No one dances that is sober—unless he happens to be crazy. What must there not be presupposed if a man so far forgets himself as to dance? As you are unable to carry your impeachment of Murena's life any further this allegation falls to the ground." (§ 13, 14, in substance.)

"Cato is a Stoic. What is a Stoic? There was once a man of supreme genius called Zeno, whose disciples call themselves Stoics.

"His principles and teaching are as follows: The wise man does nothing from personal considerations; never forgives anyone a transgression; it is only a foolish and light-minded person who is compassionate; a true man does not allow himself to yield to entreaty or to conciliation. The wise alone are beautiful, though utterly deformed; they alone are rich, though in utter beggary; they alone are kings, though they are slaves in bondage.

"But us, who are not wise, they call vagabond slaves, exiles, enemies, even madmen. All sins are equal; every shortcoming is an outrageous crime; he who wrings a fowl's neck needlessly is as great an offender as one who strangles his father.

"A wise man never *supposes* a thing, never repents, never mistakes, cannot change his mind.

"These principles an able man like Cato, allured by learned authorities, has taken up, not, as the generality do, to theorize upon, but to live by.

"Some tax-farmers come to you with a request; mind that you do not allow personal considerations to weigh with you. Some people come in sore distress and misery to entreat you; you will be an abominable criminal if you do ought for them for pity's sake. A man confesses that he has erred, and begs pardon for his offence; it is a crime to forgive. But, you urge, the transgression was a petty one. Nay, all sins are equal! You have made a statement: it is henceforth fixed and unalterable. You have been guided not by fact but by fancy; the wise man never admits a fancy. You have made a *mistake* in some matter; he thinks the word a libel.

"His arguments in our case are in the manner of his

school. 'I said in the senate that I would prosecute the candidate for the consulship.' You said it in anger. 'No,' says he, 'the wise is never angry.' But you said it to serve the moment. He replies, 'It is wicked to deceive by a lie; disgraceful to change one's mind; a crime to yield to entreaty; an enormity to pity.' Those on the contrary with whom I hold, who draw their wisdom from Plato and Aristotle, men of temper and of moderation, say that personal considerations may sometimes avail with a wise man; that to pity is the duty of a good man; that offences are not all of one kind, and that punishments must differ accordingly; that a high-principled man may sometimes forgive; that even a wise man often has an opinion on that which he does not know; that he is sometimes angry; that he is entreated and appeased; that what he has once said he will sometimes change if it is better to do so; that he does sometimes abandon his purpose; that there is a mean by which all virtues are seen to be ruled.

"If, with your natural disposition, Cato, some happy accident had brought you to the feet of these teachers, you would now be—not a better man, not of more sterling worth, more self-controlled, more upright—that could not be; but you would incline a little more to leniency. You would not, without any quarrel to incite, any wrong to provoke you, accuse a most honourable, worthy, and distinguished man; you would think that, the course of events having committed the safe-keeping of the commonwealth into Murena's hands and yours for the same year, a public tie had been established between him and you; those hard words which you let fall in the senate you would have never uttered, or you would have left them on one side or put a softer construction on them. And you yourself, so far as I may hazard a prophecy—agitated as you now are by the rush of vehement feeling, carried away by the forces of your own nature and temperament, fresh with the enthusiasm kindled in you by your favourite doctrines, will yet prove the mitigating and chastening effect of experience, of lapse of time, of riper age." * (§§ 61-65.)

---

* On Cato, the "Don Quixote of the aristocracy," and his pedantic resistance to the demands of the publicani and Pompeius, v. Mommsen iv., 1, 156, 198. Cic. says of him (ad Att. ., 1), dicit tamquam in Platonis πολιτείᾳ, non tamquam in Romuli faece, sententiam.

CHAPTER II.

Failure of Cicero's political efforts—Exile and return under the Triumvirate—Government of Cilicia—Civil war—Submission to Caesar—Last struggle in the optimate cause against Antonius—Death (B.C. 43).

U.C. 692, B.C. 62.
Oratio pro P. Cornelio Sulla.
Oratio pro Archia poeta.

IN the following year, U.C. 692, B.C. 62, Cicero defended P. Cornelius Sulla, who had been accused by L.* Torquatus of participation in Catilina's conspiracy. The prosecutor had reproached Cicero with arbitrarily at one time condemning one man on this charge, at another acquitting another. He had taunted him with being not a born Roman, but a foreigner from a *municipium*,† and at the same

---

* *V.* Dr. Reid's pro Sulla, p. 10, n. 2. It is clear that not L. Manlius T. the father (consul with Cotta, B.C. 65), but T. Manlius T., the son, was the prosecutor; the same who had accused Sulla of bribery in his canvass for the consulship. (Not so, however, Baiter and Kayser, and many other modern authorities.)

† Cp. Catilina's taunt, "M. Tullius, inquilinus civis urbis Romae."

time behaving at Rome like a king; with Numa and Tarquinius, he made the third foreign king at Rome. "Yes," replies Cicero, "I confess that I come from the *municipium* from which now for the second time deliverance has come for our city and empire. But what I should much like to know of you is why those who come from *municipia* seem to you to be foreigners?"

"No one ever uttered this reproach against the elder Marcus Cato, many enemies though he had, against Ti. Coruncanius, against M'. Curio, against my fellow-townsman Marius, though he had so many enemies." (§ 23). "Men cannot all be patricians, and if you want the truth, they do not all care to be . . . Nor am I a whit more a king than a foreigner, unless it proves one a king so to live as to be the slave of no man, and no passion either: to scorn all base desires; to covet neither gold nor silver nor ought else; to utter one's opinion freely in the senate; to regard the interests of the public rather than its wishes; to truckle to no one, to withstand many men. If this makes a king, then I confess that I am one." (§ 25, in substance.)

"It is royalty, you say, to speak against and to defend whom one will. And I say it is slavery not to speak against and to defend whom one will." (§ 48.)

In the same year* Cicero defended his friend and instructor, the poet Archias, whose claim to Roman citizenship had been disputed by one Gratius. (*Oratio pro Archia poeta.*) It was easy for the orator to prove that Archias had satisfied the *Lex Plautia Papiria de civitate*, having been a citizen of Heraclia an allied town, having been domiciled in Italy, and within the proper time having had himself entered by the praetor, Q. Metellus Pius, on the register of Roman citizens. Even if he were not a citizen, he deserved to become one on account of his talent and his services in glorifying the name of Rome. As the defence itself did not furnish much matter to the orator, he employed the opportunity of descanting in enthusiastic terms upon the subject of liberal studies,

---

* B.C. 62. Baiter and Kayser, with others, assign the speech to B.C. 61. But it was made in the court of Q. Cicero, as praetor, who in 61 was governing Asia. This we learn from a scholiast. From § 28, we know that M. Cicero's consulship was over.

still somewhat depreciated at Rome. He confesses his own predilection for the poetic art and all studies which contribute to general culture, and avows the important influence which they had exercised on his own training, and still did exercise on his practical career as a statesman and an orator.

He adduces instances to show how the greatest men had also been friends of science and art. But devotion to literature, even apart from its use in life, affords the worthiest and noblest pleasure. All other occupations are confined to some particular time of life, place, or opportunity; these studies offer to the young man the best intellectual nurture, to the old, the fairest delights; they are an ornament in prosperity, a refuge and comfort in adversity; they cheer our home life without hindering our public activity; they are the companions of our vigils, our travels, our country sojourns.

Archias is a poet. All other arts and sciences may be acquired by diligence and attention; the poet is born; he creates in virtue of an inspiration, a divine afflatus which breathes upon him. Hence Ennius properly calls poets **sacred,** as recommended to us by **a kind of Divine** bestowal. " Let then this **name of** poet," so **Cicero** addresses the judges, "which no people, however **rude, has ever** outraged, be sacred also to you as men of the highest culture. Rocks **and** wildernesses are responsive **to** his voice, savage beasts are often swayed and arrested by song ; **shall** we, who have had the highest of training, listen unmoved to the poet's voice ?

" The Colophonians say that Homer is their townsman, the Chians claim him for theirs, the Salaminians assert their title to him, the Smyrnaeans declare he belongs to them, and in that conviction have dedicated a shrine to **him** in **their town;** many more contest the honour most strenuously. And while they lay claim to a stranger, even after his death, because he **was a** poet, are we **to** disown **a** living fellow-citizen, ours by his own choice and by Roman law ? and **that** though Archias long ago devoted **all his** efforts and genius to the celebration of the glory and honour of the Roman people, the renown and honour of Rome. . . . **No one is so** unfriendly to the

Muses that he would not readily accept for his labours the immortality which the heralds of song can confer. The tale is told of Themistocles, the great Athenian, that being asked once what artiste or what singer's voice he most liked to hear, he replied : His who best proclaims my own virtue." (§§ 19, 20.)

"How many chroniclers of his exploits Alexander the Great is said to have taken with him! Yet he, when he stood beside the tomb of Achilles at Sigeum, exclaimed : O favoured youth to have found a Homer to herald your praises! True enough, for had there never been an Iliad, the same mound which covered his body would have buried his renown as well." (§ 24.)

"There is no need to dissemble what cannot be disguised ; it ought rather to be frankly avowed ; we are all impelled by the desire of praise, and the nobler the man, the more intent is he on fame. The philosophers themselves append their names to the very books which they write on the contempt of fame ; they desire to be praised and to gain a name, in regard to the very performance which con-

veys their contempt of praise and high name."
(§ 26.)

"Virtue craves no other guerdon for hardships and dangers than this of glory and renown. This once removed, gentlemen, what motive have we for all our severe exertions in this short and limited career of life? . . . A noble instinct is implanted in the heart of the best of us, which makes fame a spur to urge us night and day, and warns us that the story of our fame must not be given up to oblivion when the term of life ends, but must be made co-extensive with all future generations." (§§ 28, 29.)

"When many of the greatest men have been at pains to leave their statues and busts, the likenesses not of their souls but of their bodies, ought not we far more to wish to leave the portraiture of our aims and our virtues wrought and finished by the greatest masters? Certainly in all my actions I cherished the idea that even in the hour of doing them I was sowing and planting for myself a memory worldwide and undying.

"Whether after death this is to be foreign to my

consciousness or, as the wisest of men have thought, in some measure to come home to me, now at all events I take pleasure in some such contemplation and hope." (§ 30.)

<small>U.C. 695, B.C. 59.
Oratio pro L. Valerio Flacco.</small>

The speech for L. Valerius Flaccus belongs to the year U.C. 695, B.C. 59. Flaccus, the praetor, who had rendered Cicero such effectual service in the discovery of the Catilinarian conspiracy, had, at the instigation of Catilina's friends, been prosecuted by D. Laelius for extortion during his praetorship. Cicero's speech procured his acquittal.

Cicero's position meantime had become one of great danger. His foes had opposed his patriotic zeal with ever-increasing violence, and after Pompeius had detached himself from the senate and leagued himself with Caesar and Crassus (B.C. 60), Cicero found himself isolated. The triumvirs vainly sought to draw him over to their interest, clinging as he did to the belief that by his influence he could curb their ambition. He must, however, soon have been undeceived, when the triumvirs abandoned him to

Clodius, who brought him to account for the execution of Catilina's fellow-conspirators.* He escaped condemnation by voluntary exile in the beginning of April U.C. 696, B.C. 58.

U.C. 696, B.C. 58.
Exile of Cicero.

Clodius procured sentence of outlawry against him and the confiscation of his goods. His house at Rome was razed to the ground. His laments addressed to his friends bear witness to the depth of his dejection. In a letter to his wife, Terentia, written on the 30th of April (ad Fam. xiv, 4) occurs the following passage:

"I write less often to you than I might because, although my misery is ever present with me, yet above all when I am writing to you or reading your letters, I am so overcome by tears that I am quite

---

* Clodius as tribune brought in a law enacting "that anyone, who had put Roman citizens to death without trial, should be forbidden fire and water." The Senate, the Equites, and many thousand citizens put on mourning in sympathy with Cicero. But Pompeius refused to interfere. (Plut. Cic. 31.) It was on the very day of Cicero's voluntary departure that Clodius carried a law banishing him by name—a *privilegium*, pro Sest. § 65; *v.* Watson's Select Letters of Cicero, introd. to Part I.

unmanned. Ah, if I had only not clung so fast to life! I should then have seen but little sorrow in my life, or none at all. If fortune has reserved me for the hope of some day finding some happiness again, I have not erred so grievously; but if my present bitter fate is unalterable, then, my dearest, I could wish as soon as possible to see you and to die in your arms, since no recompense is vouchsafed us either by the gods whose pious worshipper you have been, or by men, to whose service I have ever devoted myself. . . . . Wretched, undone that I am! what shall I do? Shall I beg you, out of health, a woman broken in mind and body, to come to me? Or not ask you, and so live without you? I think it will be best thus. If there is still any hope of my return, you by your active help may promote it. But if, as I fear, all is over with me, then be sure you come to me, I care not how. One thing you must know, that if only I have you, I shall not think myself utterly ruined. For the rest, my dear Terentia, support yourself with the consoling thought that we have lived in the height of honour and in the flower of prosperity. It is no wickedness of mine, it is my virtue that has brought me to ruin. My one sin has been that I have not lost my life with my dignities. Yet if it was more agreeable to my children that I should live, let me endure all that remains, intolerable though it be. Alas, I who preach courage to you can scarcely muster any for myself!"

On the same day he writes to his friend Atticus (*ad Att.* iii. 7) : " In urging me to live, you succeed in one object, that is in keeping me from laying hands on myself; you cannot effect the other, to prevent me from regretting my resolution and my life. For what is there to keep me in life, especially if the hope which attended my departure from home is now gone? I will not attempt to recount to you all the sufferings into which the utter injustice and wickedness not so much of my enemies as of those who envy me has plunged me, that I may not arouse my grief again and invite you to the like distress. Only I maintain this, that never yet has such a misfortune befallen anyone, that never yet has anyone had better reason to pray for death. The time when I might have met it with honour has been neglected; the time that remains for me cannot heal my grief, but only set it a term."

<small>U.C. 697, B.C. 57.
Return of Cicero:
Orationes Post Reditum in Senatu: Post Reditum ad Quirites: de domo sua ad Pontifices.</small>

The exertions of his friends, especially the consul P. Lentulus Spinther, and the plebeian tribunes T. Annius Milo and P. Sestius, with the co-operation of Pompeius resulted in procuring his recall from the senate and people. His return on the 4th of September, 697 U.C., 57 B.C., was a veritable triumph. He himself writes on the subject to his friend Atticus (*ad Att.* iv. 1):

"As soon as ever I returned to Rome, and could find someone to whom I could safely commit a letter for you, I thought it my very earliest duty to give you joy of my return while you were still absent. For, to tell the truth, I had come to see that in the counsel you gave me you had shown just as little courage and discretion as I,* nor even,

---

* The alternative course for Cic. would have been to remain in Rome and defy the democrats to attack him by name. This was Lucullus' advice (Plut. Cic. 31), and would have meant a resort to arms.

considering my past attentions to you,* an excess of zeal to guard my welfare ; but that withal you, who had at the beginning shared my delusion, or rather my downright infatuation, and had associated yourself with me in my groundless fear, had felt our separation most bitterly, and had devoted the utmost zeal, pains, industry, and endeavour to accomplish my return. I can therefore truthfully assure you, that in the height of rapture, and amidst most welcome congratulations, one thing only was lacking to make my joy complete, your presence and your embrace.

"If I do but once more have you before me, and then ever let you go without exacting to the full all arrears of delight in your beloved society which I have lost, I shall surely hold myself unworthy of the restoration of my prosperity. So far I have attained, as regards my political position, what I thought almost beyond possibility of recovery, in a greater degree than I could wish, my old leadership at the

---

* Reading *nec etiam pro praeteritā mea in te observantia* with Prof. Tyrrell.

bar, and my authority in the senate, and influence with the loyalists.

"As to my private affairs, meantime (you know how they have suffered from violence, rapine, and pillage), the prospect is very gloomy, and I stand in need not so much of your resources—though I regard them as being just as much at my command as at your own—as of your counsels how we may get together and rehabilitate what is left after the general wreck. Now, although I expect that you have heard all, either by letters from your friends or by general report, I will shortly relate to you what I expect you will like to learn by letter from me rather than from any other source. On the 4th of August, I started from Dyrrhachium, the very day on which the law regarding me was brought in. I reached Brundisium on the 5th. Here I found my daughter Tullia awaiting me.

"The day was her birthday, and as it happened also the commemoration-day of the colony of Brundisium and the foundation-day of the temple of Salus, whose neighbour you are. The coincidence was noticed by the populace, and marked by the Brundisians with congratulatory demonstration. On the 8th of August, while I was still at Brundisium, I learnt by a letter from my brother Quintus that amidst extraordinary enthusiasm on the part of the citizens of every age and class, enormous crowds thronging to vote from all Italy, the law had been carried in the Comitia Centuriata. Having received various marks of respect from the leading men of Brundisium, I pursued my journey, but not without being met by deputations from every place with congratulations.

"When I arrived before Rome, my nomenclator missed not a soul known to him of any rank, who failed to come and meet me, with the exception of those enemies who could neither disguise nor disown the fact of their enmity. When I came to the Porta Capena,* the steps† of the temple were crowded from the very bottom with the common people, who

---

* Cic. had travelled by the Appian Way and thus entered the city by the Porta Capena, between the Coelian and Aventine hills: thence went by the Sacred Way to the Capitol, in a kind of triumphal procession.

† Reading *ab infimo* (Tyrrell after Lehmann).

expressed their good wishes for me by the loudest plaudits. A like multitude and a like storm of applause accompanied me to the Capitol. In the Forum too, and at the Capitol itself, the numbers assembled were surprising. . . .

"I am looking out for you, and I beg you to come with all speed, and with your mind made up not to leave me destitute of your counsel. I am now as it were beginning a new life. Meanwhile some people, who during my absence championed my cause, are already, now that I am present, beginning to harbour a sore feeling against me in private, to show their jealousy openly. I crave your presence earnestly."

On the day after his entry Cicero rendered his thanks to the senate and the people in speeches which we still possess (*Oratio post reditum in senatu habita : oratio post reditum ad Quirites habita**). In order to recover the site for rebuilding his destroyed house on the Palatine, a portion of which Clodius had dedicated

---

* This speech cannot be proved authentic by external arguments, though there is no reason to suspect it on internal grounds. The other speech, with the De domo sua ad pont. and the De harusp. responso, has been disputed also, but without success. Teuffel Hist. R. Lit. i. § 166, 30.

for the erection of a temple to Liberty, Cicero delivered at the end of the same month a speech before the pontiffs (*oratio de domo sua ad pontifices*), in which he proved the invalidity of the dedication. The college of priests, like the senate, decided in his favour, and he regained the site.

<small>U.C. 698, B.C. 56.
Oratio de haruspicum responso: pro Sestio: Interrogatio in Vatinium: Oratio pro M. Caelio: pro L. Cornelio Balbo ; de provinciis consularibus.</small>

With reference to the same affair, Cicero in the following year delivered in the senate against Clodius the speech *De haruspicum responso*. Clodius, in a popular assembly, had interpreted in reference to the building of Cicero's house a declaration of the soothsayers, that hallowed places had been desecrated ; Cicero on the contrary applies the utterance to Clodius' own enormities.

If Cicero after his return was from the outset allied to Pompeius by feelings of gratitude, the dread of the persecutions of Clodius and the conviction of the powerlessness of the senate drove him more and more into his arms. On several occasions, too, he showed complaisance to Caesar.

"As those who have no power," he writes to Atticus (*ad Att.* iv. 5), "will not love me, let us try to make ourselves well-beloved of those who have power. You will say, That is what I could have wished to see long ago. I know that you wished it, and that I have been a downright ass.* But it is high time for me to bestow on myself the love that I cannot get from my former friends." As his political activity was crippled by the power of the triumvirs, he devoted his energies with all the more zeal to the forum, in the defence of his friends persecuted by his political adversaries.

In the year U.C. 698, B.C. 56, P. Sestius was accused by M. Tullius Albinovanus of having raised disturbances in favour of Cicero's recall. Cicero undertook the defence, detailing at full length the intrigues and the lawless violence of his adversaries, especially of Clodius, and showing how Sestius, as tribune at the time had acted only in the interest of the state, and of the speaker's righteous cause.

---

* "Me asinum germanum fuisse." The epithet implies mulishness and a thick skin, rather than stupidity.

Sestius was unanimously acquitted. Connected with the speech of Sestius is the *interrogatio in Vatinium*, a refutation of Vatinius, who had come forward as a witness against Sestius. His political career, more especially during his tribunate, is shown up in a vivid light.

The speech for **Caelius** (*oratio pro M. Caelio*) likewise belongs to this year. M. Caelius Rufus was a friend of Cicero's, and honoured him as his teacher and patron.

He had prosecuted L. Atratinus for corrupt practices (*ambitus*), upon which Atratinus, son of the former, accused him of having borrowed money from Clodia, the notorious sister of P. Clodius, to procure the assassination of Dio, the Egyptian envoy, and of having thereafter attempted to poison Clodia. Cicero refutes the charge, admitting indeed that Caelius was a young man of somewhat dissolute character, but showing that the alleged offence, of which an otherwise noble youth was incapable, was the joint fabrication of his enemies, to whom the infamous Clodia lent a hand, because the defendant, taken in her toils in the thoughtlessness of youth, had determined to break loose from her. Caelius was acquitted.

About the same time Cicero defended L. Cornelius Balbus (*oratio pro L. Cornelio Balbo*), a favourite of Pompeius and notably also of Caesar, whose citizenship, conferred on him by Pompeius, it was sought to dispute. He also delivered in the senate the speech *de provinciis consularibus*,* in which he recommended that the two Gauls should be left under Caesar's command, that the present governors should be recalled from Syria and Macedonia, and these provinces assigned to the outgoing consuls.

Piso, recalled in consequence from Macedonia by the senate, made a violent attack on Cicero, who

---

* Cic. had been encouraged by a temporary coolness between Pompeius and Crassus, and by the success of his attack on Vatinius, a creature of Caesar's, to oppose the triumvirs: in particular proposing to discuss the Julian land-law in the senate. The conference of the triumvirs at Luca, attended by 200 senators, settled their differences. Cicero had to withdraw from his attitude of opposition; he alludes to his "eating humble pie" (subturpicula παλινῳδία) in *ad Att.* iv. 5, quoted above in part. This "recantation" was probably the speech *de prov. consularibus*.

replied in the speech against Piso (*in L. Pisonem*), delivered in the senate, U.C. 699, B.C. 55, in which Piso's life, both public and private, is painted in the darkest colours.

U.C. 699, B.C. 55.
Oratio in L. Calpurnium Pisonem.

In the following year Cicero defended Cn. Plancius (*Oratio pro Cn. Plancio*), who at the time of his flight to Macedonia had received and sheltered him against the prosecution of M. Juventius Laterensis for having used unlawful means in his candidature for the aedileship. Laterensis, who had brought the charge because he had himself been unsuccessful in the contest, was himself as well as Plancius a friend of Cicero's, and had alleged against the orator that in his excess of gratitude to Plancius he had violated the duties of friendship toward himself. Cicero replies thus: "Your stake in the trial, Laterensis, is

U.C. 700, B.C. 54.
Oratio pro Cn. Plancio;
pro M. Aemilio Scauro;
pro C. Rabirio Postumo.*

---

* In the same year he submitted to the humiliation of defending his former enemies, creatures of the triumvirs, Vatinius and Gabinius.

nothing more than your cherished ambition, or, if you insist upon it, your reputation, and the distinction of the aedileship; with Plancius, civic existence, country, possessions are at stake. You have wished my welfare: Plancius has made it possible. Yet I feel my heart torn by distracting emotions: I am grieved that, in a contest of such unequal interests, I must fall foul of you. But before heaven, I would rather sacrifice for you my own welfare than surrender that of Plancius* as a prey to your animosity.

"For, gentlemen of the jury, if I wish myself the possession of any virtue at all, there is nothing which I should sooner wish than gratitude, alike the appearance of it and the reality. This particular virtue is not only the highest virtue, but it is the mother of all virtues. What else is filial affection than grateful goodwill to parents? What are good citizens, those who in war and peace deserve well of their country, save those who gratefully remember their country's kindnesses? What else are pious and devout men

---

* Or "to a mere comparison of your respective merits" (following Holden).

than those who discharge their debt of gratitude to the immortal gods by proper solemnities and thankful recollection? What attractions has life without friendships? And how can friendship exist between the ungrateful? Who amongst us, that has received a liberal training, does not cherish in his heart with grateful remembrance the thought of his foster-fathers, teachers, and masters, and even of the place, inarticulate instructor as it is, where he was nursed and taught? Who can possess, who ever did possess, such resources as to be able to stand without the good services of many friends, services which assuredly can never come into existence if you do away with memory and gratitude? Yes, I believe there is nothing so characteristic of true humanity as the bond which is knit not merely by good service rendered, but even by good-will intimated; nothing, on the other hand, which is so repugnant to humanity, so monstrous and brutish, as to allow oneself to appear, I will not say unworthy of kindness, but outdone by it's magnitude." (§§ 79-81.)

Beside the speech, in part extant, for M. Aemilius

Scaurus, who was prosecuted for acts of extortion and violence committed by him in Sardinia as propraetor, the speech for C. Rabirius Postumus belongs also to this year.

This Rabirius, son of C. Curius and adopted son of C. Rabirius, whom Cicero had previously defended had with Gabinius been accused of extortion in Egypt, and sentenced to give part compensation. Cicero undertook the vindication of Rabirius more because the latter had helped to procure his recall from exile than because he was convinced of the justice of his case. In fact the defence was too weak to be of any avail, and Rabirius went into exile.

<small>U.C. 702, B.C. 52. Oratio pro T. Annio Milone.</small> Equally unfortunate was the defence of Milo (*oratio pro T. Annio Milone*), Cicero's friend, and the stubborn opponent of Clodius, whom he had killed on the road to Lanuvium in January U.C. 702, B.C. 52.

The populace, exasperated by the death of Clodius, raised disturbances, in consequence of which Pompeius, elected sole consul, instituted the judicial enquiry, after having modified for such cases the usual form of procedure. The prosecutors of Milo were Appius Claudius, a nephew of the deceased, M. Antonius and P. Valerius Nepos; Cicero undertook the defence. The forum and the neighbouring streets were held by troops during the proceedings, and Pompeius in person presided, sitting in front of the Treasury surrounded by a picked body of soldiers.

Cicero is said to have so completely lost his self-command at the noise and clamour of Clodius' partisans, that his speech proved a failure, and Milo was condemned. The latter retired into voluntary exile at Massilia. Cicero afterwards re-wrote his speech. The proem of the speech as originally delivered survived to Quintilian's time (iv. 3,17). The elaborated speech which we now possess is described by Quintilian (iv. 2, 25 ; xi. 3, 47) as the finest and most famous of all those of Cicero, and Asconius considers it the most admirable, as having been composed with all the perfection of a master's hand.*
Milo on reading it is said to have exclaimed, "If

---

* Scripsit hanc, quam legimus, ita perfecte, ut iure prima haberi possit. *Argum. Ascon. ad or. p. M.*

Cicero had spoken thus in court, I should not have been eating these fine mullets of Marseilles."*

The speech begins with an exhortation to the judges. The new form of procedure and the military precautions would inspire him with anxiety, did he not count on Pompeius' wisdom and justice and the sympathy of the citizens assembled in such numbers; the judges accordingly may dismiss all fear, mindful of their duty, and intent only on the safety of Milo, a man who had deserved so well of them. Milo has slain Clodius; but it is not the case that everyone who has slain a man is a murderer, and liable to death. Horatius slew his sister, and yet the people acquitted him. Publius Africanus, when asked what he thought of the death of Tiberius Gracchus, said that it seemed to him that he had been rightfully slain.

And so the history of Rome displayed many examples of agitators who had been slain without their death being imputed as a crime to its authors.

---

* *Dio Cassius* xl. 54.

Yes, the goddess of wisdom herself had acquitted Orestes of matricide, because he had been avenging his father's death. The ordinances of the senate and of nature warrant homicide in self-defence. Milo too has used weapons only in self-defence. The act then is not a public offence, as Milo's enemies would make out. If it were such, the senate and Pompeius would have condemned Milo instead of instituting an enquiry. Clodius, who was standing for the praetorship, but knew that if Milo were made consul he would be unable to prosecute his criminal designs against the state, had often declared that if the consulship could not be taken from Milo, his life could be taken.

He knew that Milo had to journey to Lanuvium for the nomination of a flamen on the 20th of January. He himself suddenly left Rome the day before, in order to lay an ambush before his own farm to entrap Milo. Milo was still in the senate on this day, and, as soon as it broke up, went to his house, changed his shoes and his clothes, and had to wait some time longer, because his wife, as usually happens, could not so soon complete her preparations for the journey.* He then started just at the time when Clodius might have already been back if he had meant to be in Rome on the same day. They met on the way, Clodius without baggage, on horseback, without a train of Greeks, a thing quite unusual with him, without his wife, a thing almost unprecedented; while the alleged assassin, Milo, was riding with his wife in a coach, wrapped in a travelling-cloak, with a quantity of baggage, and attended by a large train of weak maidservants and page-boys. He fell in with Clodius before his estate about the eleventh hour. Suddenly he was attacked by a number of persons with missiles from higher ground, while another party killed the coachman. Upon this, while Milo threw off his cloak, sprang from the coach, and courageously defended himself, Clodius' retinue drew their swords; some ran back to the coach in order to attack Milo in the rear, others believing him to be already killed began to cut down his slaves who were behind. Such of these as were loyal to their master

---

* Halm quotes Ter. Heaut. ii. 1, 10; nosti mores mulierum: dum moliuntur, dum comuntur, annus est.

and kept their presence of mind were some of them killed, while others, seeing the fight go on beside the coach, prevented from helping their master, hearing from Clodius' own lips that Milo was slain, and supposing it to be the fact, without orders or knowledge or even presence of their master did what every one of us would have wished his servants to do in such a case. Such is a statement of the facts. The question is, who had the greater interest in the death of the other? For Clodius, everything turned on the death of Milo, if he was to hope to carry out his designs against the state; while Milo could only lose rather than gain by the death of Clodius.

The hatred of Clodius against Milo, the crimes of his previous life, his expectation of impunity for the murder, his repeated menacing declarations, the place, the occasion, all the circumstances of the incident, speak to the fact of his having intended to kill Milo.

On the other hand it proves the innocence of Milo, that he has returned to Rome, despising all the rumours disseminated about him; for he knew that he had delivered the state from a monster, as the joy of the Roman people at the death of Clodius attested.

His act is therefore worthy of praise rather than of punishment; and to the fortune of the Roman people and to the immortal gods our thanks for this benefit are due.

"Do you, then," says Cicero in conclusion, "accord to a gallant man that pity which he does not entreat, but which I, in his despite, entreat and demand for him. If he, while none of us can refrain from weeping, has not shed one tear; if you see no change in his face or his voice, do not judge him the more severely; it is a proof of his strength of soul." (§ 92, in substance.) "He believes that there alone is exile, where there is no room for virtue, that death is the natural ending, not a punishment. This is his inborn temper of mind. But you, judges, what is your resolve to be? Will you preserve the memory of Milo, while you banish himself? What place in the world can be fitter to harbour such merit than that which gave it birth? To you, I appeal, to you, brave men, who have often shed your blood for the country, to you, centurions and soldiers, in this hour of a dauntless man's danger, your fellow-citizen; under your gaze, ay, while under arms you mount guard over this court, is such merit as this to be banished the city, expatriated, cast adrift? Ill-fated, unhappy man that I am! You, Milo, by means of the men before me could recall me to my country; and shall I be unable by their means to retain you in that country? What answer shall I make to my children, who look on you as a second father? What to you, my brother Quintus, now absent, my partner in those times of trial? That I should have failed to maintain Milo's safety by the help of the very men by whom he retrieved mine! Failed, and in what a cause? In one which commands ready and universal support. Failed, by the verdict of whom?* Of those who found the greatest relief in Clodius' death. Failed, upon whose intercession? My own. What great crime did I commit, of what enormity was I guilty, judges, when I tracked out, revealed, exposed,

---

* Reading with Madvig *quae est grata gentibus omnibus. At quibus iudicantibus non potuisse?*

and stifled in the germ the indications which threatened universal destruction? That is the source from which gush all the sorrows that I and mine have known. Why did you decree my return? That those should be banished under my eyes to whom my restoration was due? Do not, I entreat you, do not suffer my return to be a greater bitterness than even my departure; how can I think myself restored if I am torn from those to whom I owe my restoration? Would that heaven had granted (forgive the utterance, my country, for I fear that the language of devotion to Milo may savour of blasphemy to thee) that Clodius were not only alive, but even were praetor, consul, dictator, rather than I should see this sight! Ye powers above! a gallant man is this, and one whom it behoves you, gentlemen of the jury, to save! 'Not so, not so,' I hear him say; 'enough that the dead has paid the penalty due; let me, if needs be, undergo what is not due.' Shall a man like this, born for his country, die elsewhere than in his country, or, if so it chance, for his country? Will you treasure the memorials of his spirit, but allow his body no burial in Italy? Will anyone by his vote banish from the city a man to whom, banished by you, all cities will offer a welcome? Happy that land that shall harbour a man like this; ungrateful ours, if she cast him out; unhappy, if she lose him! But enough: I can indeed no longer speak for tears, and Milo will not have tears employed in his defence. You, judges, I pray and entreat, in recording your verdict, to show the courage of your convictions. And, believe me, he who in the choice of jurors has selected only the best, wisest, and bravest, will be most likely to approve your manliness, uprightness, and loyalty." * (§§ 101-105.)

U.C. 703. B.C. 51.
Cicero Proconsul of Cilicia.

In May, U.C. 703, B.C. 51, Cicero proceeded to Cilicia as proconsul. He describes to his friend Atticus the melancholy situation in which he had found the country. Lamentation, complaints, and im-

---

* Referring to Pompeius, whose attitude as a matter of fact turned the verdict against Milo.

poverishment met him on every side. "In short," he writes, "people are universally disgusted with life. Some relief, however, has been afforded to the unfortunate towns by my sparing them all charges for myself, my legates, the quaestor, or anyone whatever. You must know that we not only decline fodder for our horses, and the usual allowances under the Lex Julia,* but even wood; and that we will not any of us accept anything beyond four beds and a roof, in fact in many places not so much as a roof, but we lodge in a tent. You cannot imagine how the people flock in to see us from the country places,

---

* A law of Caesar's first consulship, forbidding provincial governors when travelling to claim anything without compensation but wood, salt, and hay (*Watson's Letters of Cic.* 32). The Cyprians had paid Appius Claudius, Cicero's predecessor, 200 Attic talents in order not to have soldiers quartered on them (*ad Att.* v. 21, 7). Cic. prides himself also on accepting no substantial honours, such as shrines and statues, from the Cilicians. His friend M. Caelius Rufus importunes him (in vain, as it seems) to send him panthers to exhibit in the arena, as he was standing for the aedileship. But in the case of the extortioner Scaptius Cic. took a weakly neutral course (*ad Att.* v. 21, 12). "When the *ordinum concordia* and the natural rights of the province had to be weighed against each other, the latter kicked the beam." *V. Quarterly Review*, October, 1888, Cicero's Government of Cilicia.

the villages, and houses everywhere. They are really coming to life again, thanks to my arrival, thanks to the uprightness, disinterestedness, and forbearance of your Cicero. So completely has he surpassed all expectations!" (*Ad Att.* v. 16.)

Cicero also won military renown. He marched against the bandit population of mount Amanus, and was hailed Imperator by his troops. With a good deal of humour he relates this episode to his friend Atticus (v. 20): "On the Saturnalia, early in the morning the people of Pindenissus surrendered, the fifty-seventh day after the siege began. 'Who the mischief are your Pindenissians? who are they?' you will say; 'I never heard the name.' What am I to do? Pray could I change Cilicia into Aetolia or Macedonia? . . From Iconium, where alarming intelligence about the Parthians reached me, I pushed forward into Cilicia through the part of Cappadocia which borders on it, on purpose that Artavasdes the Armenian and the Parthians themselves should believe themselves to be cut off from Cappadocia. After a five-days' halt in camp at Cybistra tidings came that the Parthians were at a long distance from this approach to Cappadocia, and were now rather threatening Cilicia itself. Hereupon I marched at speed into Cilicia through the pass of Mount Taurus. I arrived at Tarsus on the fifth of October; thence I started for Mount Amanus, which forms the watershed between Syria and Cilicia, and was occupied by a permanently hostile population. Here on the thirteenth of October we killed a large number of the enemy. After Pomptinus had arrived at night and I early in the morning we took and burnt their strongly-fortified castles. I was hereupon hailed as Imperator. We occupied a camp here for several days, the same in fact which Alexander once held, at Issus, against Darius—a general not a little superior to you or me. We remained on the spot five days, and after we had sacked and devastated Mount Amanus, we retired. You know of course what the Greek calls a 'panic' and 'the idle fears of war.' At the report of our arrival, Cassius also, who had been pent within the walls of Antioch, took courage, and the Parthians took alarm. They retired from the city, and Cassius pursued and gained some advantage over them. In the flight Osaces, the influential leader of the Parthians, received a wound, of which he died within a few days. My name is in high favour in Syria. Meantime Bibulus arrived. I think he wished not to stand behind me in this empty title of Imperator. He wished at the same Amanus to win, as the saying is, 'a sprig of bay in a wedding-cake.'* But he lost the whole of the first cohort, and Asinius Dento, centurion of the first rank, a man of renown in his own degree, the others of the same cohort, and Sex. Lucilius, a military tribune, son of Gavius Caepio, a man of wealth and distinction. The loss of such a man at such time was a sharp rap on the knuckles. We hereupon marched upon Pindenissus, which was in arms, the most strongly fortified town of the Eleuthero-Cilicians within the memory of man—a wild and warlike people, provided with all means of defence. We invested them with trench and rampart, a huge

---

* Laureolam in mustaceo quaerere, to win a cheap renown.

mound, mantlets, a very high tower, a large train of siege-artillery, and a strong force of archers, in fact with all exertion and military appliances. At the cost of a good many wounded, but without reverse to the army as a whole, we have accomplished what we undertook. Naturally, a merry Saturnalia followed, especially for the soldiers, to whom I made over the booty with the exception of the horses. The prisoners were offered for sale on the third day of the Saturnalia."

The *Epp. ad Fam.*, xv. 1-4, give more detailed accounts addressed to Cato and the senate.*

U.C. 704, B.C. 50. Return from Cilicia to Italy.
In July, U.C. 704, B.C. 50, Cicero began his return journey to Italy, where he arrived at the end of No-

---

* Mommsen's criticism on the correspondence of Cic. may here be noted:—" People are in the habit of calling it interesting and clever; and it is so, as long as it reflects the urban or villa life of the world of quality; but where the writer is thrown on his own resources, as in exile, in Cilicia, and after the battle of Pharsalus, it is stale and empty as ever was the soul of a feuilletonist banished from his familiar circles." Momms. iv. ii. p. 609.

vember. The contest for supreme power in the state soon afterwards broke out between Caesar and Pompeius (U.C. 705, B.C. 49); and Cicero hesitated long whose side he should join. He at length decided for Pompeius, repaired to Capua, and thence to Greece, but from ill-health took no part in the battle of Pharsalus, U.C. 706, B.C. 48, and after the fight of Pompeius refused to assume the command of the fleet.

On his return to Italy, he was compelled to wait nearly a whole year at Brundisium until Caesar, who treated him with great consideration and friendliness, being on his way back from Egypt, gave him permission to return to Rome. He now withdrew from all public activity; only occasionally did he open his lips in defence of friends in jeopardy.

U.C. 708, B.C. 46.
Oratio pro M. Marcello.

In reference to the recall of M. Marcellus, who had belonged to the Pompeian party, a concession granted by Caesar to the urgent prayer of the senate, Cicero spoke again in the senate-house, for the first time after a long interval.* The speech consists mainly of a declamatory eulogium upon Caesar, which afterwards served the younger Pliny as a model for his panegyric upon Trajan.

<small>Oratio pro Q. Ligario.</small> In the defence of Q. Ligarius,† which Cicero delivered in the same year in the forum before Caesar, he is again quite the orator of old. Q. Ligarius was before the outbreak of the war legate of the propraetor Considius in Africa, who, on leaving the province, committed to him the conduct of affairs. During the civil war, being called upon by the party of Pompeius in Africa

---

* Statueram non mehercule inertia sed desiderio pristinae dignitatis *in perpetuum tacere* (ad fam. iv. 4, 4). A resolve which Cicero was not likely to keep. The speech in which he broke silence has been characterised as servile in its fulsomeness. But it was delivered under the influence of intense emotion—speciem aliquam videbar videre quasi reviviscentis rei publicae (ad fam. iv. 4, 3). His despair had been succeeded by hopes not to be realised. The elasticity of his nature explains much.

† This speech, the *pro Marcello*, and the *pro rege Deiotaro* are included by the old grammarians under the common title of Caesarianae, 'speeches delivered before Caesar.' The genuineness of the *pro Marc.* was denied by F. A. Wolf, mainly on linguistic grounds, which seem untenable.

to become their leader, he declined. Meantime P. Attius Varus came to Africa as a fugitive, and assumed the chief command.

Under direction from him Ligarius refused to Aelius Tubero, the rightful governor of the province, not only permission to land himself, but even to set on shore his sick son Quintus.

Afterwards, when the relations and friends of Ligarius, who had been captured after the battle of Thapsus and sent into exile, endeavoured with Cicero's support to procure from Caesar his recall, this Q. Tubero, who like his father had after the battle of Pharsalus forsaken the cause of Pompeius and had been spared by Caesar, opposed them. To this end he brought forward a charge against Ligarius on the ground of his continued stay in Africa, seeking to represent him as possessed with a special animosity against Caesar,—an accusation which Cicero turns into ridicule.

He thus begins his speech: "A strange sort of charge, and one hitherto unknown, Caesar, has my kinsman Q. Tubero brought before your tribunal;—that

Q. Ligarius was in Africa! And in fact C. Pansa, a man of eminent ability, on the strength perhaps of the intimacy which he enjoys with you, has ventured to admit as much. So that I did not know which way to turn; for I had come prepared, on the supposition that you did not know the fact, and could not have learnt it from anyone else, to take advantage of your ignorance for the relief of a friend in distress.

"But since his adversary's industry has tracked out what was a secret, I must, I suppose, admit the point, especially as my good friend Pansa has already by his action taken the matter out of my hands; I must put aside argument, and address my speech entirely to your compassion, to which so many owe their preservation, who have won from you not an acquittal from guilt, but a condonation of error. You have then, Tubero, that which an advocate above everything desires, a defendant who admits the charge, but who in so doing only admits that he was on the same side as yourself, and as one who merits every praise that can be given, your own father. You will therefore both have to acknowledge **your own** delinquency before you can take exception to any shortcoming on the **part** of Ligarius." (§§ **1, 2.**) **Further, to** have belonged to Pompeius' **party can be no** crime.

"Some put it down to error, **some to fear;** less lenient judges, to hope, ambition, enmity, irreconcilable temper; the severest, to recklessness; a crime, save you, no one yet has called it. **For my** part, if the **true** and proper description of our misfortune is in question, it would seem as **if it was a** sudden fatality that blinded men's better judgment, so that none need wonder that human counsels were overborne by the irresistible will of heaven.

"**Be** it granted that we are wretched; though with such **a** conqueror we cannot well **be** so; but I am not speaking of ourselves, but of those who have fallen: say that they **were** ambitious, were passionate, irreconcilable; but the charge of crime, blind passion, parricidal treason—from these the dead Pompeius **and many more may** well be exempt. When did anyone hear a word of this from you, Caesar? What purpose had your arms beyond repelling affront?* What was the aim of your invincible army, save to maintain its own rights and your dignity? In desiring to preserve peace, were you endeavouring to arrive at a compromise with criminals, or with loyal citizens? For my part, Caesar, your high claims upon my gratitude would certainly appear to be lessened, if I thought that I had been spared by you as a criminal. Or where would your claims upon the gratitude of the republic come in, if the many men, whom you have chosen to leave undisturbed in their dignities, were one and all criminals? In your view, Caesar, it was at the outset a secession, not a war; a rupture between citizens, not the enmity of foes, in which both parties sought the country's good, but from error of judgment or predilections, missed

---

* A direct attack had been aimed at C. in two ways by the *Lex Pompeia de iure magistratuum*: it required candidates for office to stand for it *in person* (C. was in Gaul): it made him liable to be succeeded in his province on March 1st, 49 B.C., instead of waiting for a successor to the end of that year. For this, and the subsequent debates in the Senate, v. Mommsen, iv, II., p. 350, ff.: Momms. abr. p. 443 ff.

the common welfare. The chiefs were of well-nigh equal worth, not so perhaps their followers; the just cause was doubtful for the time being, because either side had something in its case which it could make good; whereas now that cause must be pronounced the better which heaven itself has espoused;* and with our experience of your clemency, who can fail to approve a victory in which no man has fallen except in the field?" (§§ 17-19.)

Cicero concludes thus: "The course which you lately took in the senate-house respecting the noble and distinguished M. Marcellus, I ask you now to take in the forum in respect to these worthy men, brothers pleading for a brother with the support of this crowded audience. As you yielded the one to the senate's entreaties, grant the other to those of the people, by whose wishes you have ever set the highest store. If that day brought you the highest renown, and the people of Rome the utmost satisfaction, I beg you, Caesar, to neglect no opportunity of

---

* Victrix causa deis placuit; sed victa Catoni (Lucan i. 128).

winning a similar glory. There is nothing that conciliates popular favour like kindheartedness; none of your many virtues that commands more admiration and gratitude than does your mercifulness. There is nothing in which mankind more nearly approach divinity, than in granting deliverance to their fellows. The greatness of your fortune consists in the fact that you have the power, the goodness of your heart in the fact that you have the will to save as many men as possible." (§ 37.)

Ligarius upon this was pardoned by Caesar.

Eulogy upon Cato Uticensis. In the same year Cicero wrote a eulogy upon Cato Uticensis, under the title of *Cato*. "As for the *Cato*," he writes to Atticus (xii. 4), "it is an Archimedean problem. I cannot manage to write what your guests (friends of Caesar's) can read with pleasure or even patience. In fact even if I were inclined to compose a bald panegyric upon his austerity and strength of character, without any reference to his characteristic sayings or to his general policy and aims, this too would be but sorry hearing for them.

But the man cannot truly be eulogised unless the fact be shown, in its proper setting, that he not only foresaw the present state of things, but also did his utmost to prevent it, and quitted life rather than see it realised."

It was not wonderful that Caesar found himself impelled, in his own vindication, to compose his *Anti Cato*. Both writings are lost, as likewise the panegyric upon Porcia, Cato's sister (*Porciae laudatio*), which Cicero composed in the following year.

U.C. 709, B.C. 45.
Oratio pro rege Deiotaro.

In the year U.C. 709, B.C. 45, Cicero defended Deiotarus, king of Galatia, who had become his friend, at Caesar's own house. Deiotarus, who had joined Pompeius, and fought under him at Pharsalus, was afterwards pardoned by Caesar, who, on his march to Pontus, visited him, and was hospitably entertained. Deiotarus meantime had been compelled to quit Armenia.

Two years later, Saocondarius, the king's son-in-

---

* Ad Att. xiii. 37-48.

law, sent his son Castor to Rome, who accused his grandfather of having attempted Caesar's life during his sojourn with him; and the physician Phidippus, a servant of Deiotarus, supported the charge. Cicero, in the opening of his speech, apologises for the nervousness which in some degree always affected him in beginning a speech,* but was mainly due to the fact that he was for the first time defending a king, and that upon a charge on which the very man against whom the alleged attempt was said to have been made was to judge—although on the other hand he was reassured by the penetration and the equity of Caesar. Lastly, the place where he was to plead was somewhat strange to him. "For," he continues (§§ 6, 7), "if I were defending this case, Caesar, in the forum (still in your hearing and before your tribunal), what encouragement would the throng of Roman citizens afford me! For which of them would not make cause with the king, whom he remembered to

---

* Cp. Cluent. § 51. In de orat. i. § 120 Cic. notes this nervousness as a mark of the best orator.

have spent his whole life in the wars of the Roman people! I should view the senate-house, should gaze on the forum, yes, should appeal to the heaven above my head. Then, when I recalled the benefits which the immortal gods, the Roman people and senate have conferred on the king, words could not possibly fail me. But confined as I am by the walls of a room, my delivery cramped by my environment, it is for you, Caesar, to estimate by your own extensive experience of defence what my feelings are, so that your fair-mindedness and your patient attention may lessen this embarrassment of mine."

The enemies of Deiotarus, the orator explains, have hoped that Caesar has a grudge against the king, and will therefore find their falsehoods credible; but Caesar cherishes no grudge, being naturally placable, and being convinced of the innocence of Deiotarus, who espoused the cause of Pompeius only because he was misled by false reports, and afterwards expiated his error by the services which he rendered to Caesar in the Alexandrine war. The accusation that Deiotarus had sought to procure Caesar's murder during his stay with him, breaks down at once in view of the monstrous nature of the act, with which a man of the kindly character and proved uprightness of Deiotarus cannot be credited ; further, the locality and the way in which (as was alleged) the deed was to be carried out manifestly reveal the charge as due to an intrigue among the ambitious relatives of the king. Otherwise, how could the king have sent Phidippus, being privy to the deed, to Rome ? In the same way the statements of the prosecution about the large army which the king was said to have prepared, about his dislike to Caesar, his wild and dissolute life, the alleged reports of his agents as to Caesar's unpopularity at Rome, and his own resentment about the loss of Armenia, were a tissue of falsehoods.

"If the orator's defence," so Cicero concludes, "is prompted by friendship towards a king who had deserved well of himself and of the state, Caesar in his verdict will be guided by no grudge, but by his well-known clemency. It is a king and his son, who as suppliants seek his mercy. And the name of king has always been sacred in this state ; but most

sacred, those of kings our friends and allies."
(§ 41.)

"I would therefore have you consider, Caesar, that to-day your decision carries with it for a royal house either hopeless ruin along with utter ignominy, or untarnished honour with **security**; the accusers are so cruel as to desire the former alternative; **your** clemency should establish the latter."

The result of the speech was that Caesar provisionally **adjourned** the case*; his death prevented a definite decision.

The enforced leisure **to** which Cicero was condemned by circumstances, he employed in the composition of philosophical works, the greater part of which was produced at this time. "I have written more," he himself says (*de Off.* iii. 4), "**in** the short time since **the** overthrow of the constitution than **in** the many years during which the republic **existed**."

---

* This is a mere conjecture. On the news of Caesar's death, D. immediately recovered Lesser Armenia by force of arms; his envoys at Rome meanwhile procured from Antonius a forged order of Caesar's, that **it was** to **be** restored to him. *Phil.* ii., §§ 94, **95.**

Caesar's murder on the 15th of March, U.C. 710, B.C. 44, once more interrupted his leisure. Cicero, who probably was not privy to the plot, approved the deed notwithstanding.*

<small>U.C. 710, B.C. 44.
Murder of Julius Caesar.
First, Second, Third, and Fourth Philippics.</small>

He proposed in the senate a general amnesty, which was carried. Ere long the intrigues of Antonius and the threats of Caesar's adherents compelled him to leave Rome.

He was already travelling towards Greece, when false reports of Antonius' coming round induced him to return to the capital. On the very day after his arrival Antonius made him feel his enmity and unbounded caprice. Cicero, on the plea of fatigue from

---

* Cicero's verdict is summed up in a letter to Atticus: "Alas, I fear that the Ides of March have brought us nothing more than the gratification of our hatred and our vengeance: ὦ πράξεως καλῆς μὲν, ἀτελοῦς δὲ" (ad Att. xiv. 12). So he writes to the conspirators, "I wish you had invited me to the banquet of the Ides of March; assuredly if you had no fragments would have been left" (ad Fam. x. 28; xii. 4).—This implies that Cic. was not in the plot—"O merciful gods! the tyrant is slain, but tyranny yet lives" (ad Att. xiv. 9, written April 17, 44 B.C.).

travel and indisposition, had absented himself from a meeting of the senate, in which the establishment of a perpetual thanksgiving in Caesar's honour was to be decreed, on the proposal of Antonius, and the latter threatened to have him fetched by force. This provoked Cicero to deliver against him in the senate on the following day (Sept. 2, 710, B.C. 44) the *First Philippic.** In it he accounts for his absence and his return; confesses that he had advised the ratification of Caesar's ordinances, in so far as they were for the good of the commonwealth, but taxes Antonius with employing alleged ordinances of Caesar to cover his own arbitrary proceedings, and with surrounding himself with armed men, professedly as a bodyguard, but evidently in order to overawe everyone else.

"Whence, then, this great and sudden change? I cannot bring myself to think that you were bribed to it. Anyone may say what he pleases, but one is not bound to believe it; for I never witnessed in you

---

* So called after the Philippics of Demosthenes; probably by Cic. himself (Plut. Cic. xlviii.). But this title first appears in Juv. x. 125 te conspicuae, divina Philippica, famae.

anything mean or low. . . . . What I do rather fear is that, blind to the true path of glory, you may think it a glorious thing to hold in your hands the sole power without a rival, and to be dreaded by your fellow-citizens. If this is your idea you are an utter stranger to the path of glory. To be beloved as a citizen, to deserve well of the commonwealth, to be eulogized, honoured, esteemed—this is glorious; but to be dreaded and hated is an ungrateful and unhallowed lot, a frail and precarious condition. As we see even on the stage that the sentiment 'Let them hate so only they fear' proved the ruin of him who uttered it. Would that you remembered your grandfather, Antonius, though you have often enough heard me speak of him at length. Think you that he would have wished to earn an immortality at the price of being dreaded on the score of a free leave to maintain a bodyguard? This he felt was true life, was true prosperity, to be the equal of his fellows in freedom, their chief in moral worth. And therefore, leaving out of account your grandfather's successes, I would prefer that last day of his, untimely as it befell him, to the tyranny of Lucius Cinna, by whom he was barbarously put to death.

"But why seek to sway you by words? If Caesar's ending cannot induce you to prefer being beloved to being feared, no words of man will profit or avail aught. Those who think that he was happy are themselves miserable. None is happy who lives under such conditions, that the man who takes his life far from being punished earns the highest glory by the deed. I beg you then change your course; look to the example of your ancestors, and so steer the ship of state that your countrymen may have reason to rejoice, not sorrow, that you were born." (§§ 33-35.)

Antonius revenged himself by a speech in which he attacked the whole of Cicero's political career. The latter wrote in reply to Antonius' invectives the *Second Philippic*, which contains the most violent attacks upon him. He first sent it to Atticus. "Ah! How I fear what you will think of it," he writes (*ad Att.* xv. 13). "Still, what can it matter to me? as it shall not see the light until the republic is recovered." Atticus approved the speech (*ad Att.*

xvi. 11), but Cicero did not dare to publish it till Antonius had left Rome. "To what destiny of mine am I to ascribe the fact that no enemy has arisen against the state during the last twenty years, who has not also at the same time declared war against me? I need not name any one of them; you have only to call them up in memory for yourselves.

"To me they have made even a fuller expiation than I could have wished. I am amazed that you, Antonius, do not dread the fate of those whose conduct you emulate. In the case of the others, it was less surprising to me; none of them was my enemy of his own choice, they were all attacked by me on political grounds. But you, never offended by me in a single word, have nevertheless, as though to show yourself more audacious than Catilina, more frenzied than Clodius, gone out of your way to attack me with abuse, and believed that your estrangement from me would be a recommendation for you with traitorous citizens. Am I then to suppose that you found something in myself to despise? I do not see what Antonius can find so contemptible in my life, my influence, my achievements, the moderate talents which I possess. Or did he think to disparage me more easily in the senate than elsewhere? But this order has given the most famous citizens an attestation of their having well governed the state, to me alone of having saved it. Or was he bent on entering the lists against me as a public speaker? That were a kindness indeed. Could there be a richer and more fertile theme, than I shall have in speaking for myself and against Antonius?

"No, that was the true reason: he thought the one way to approve himself to his compeers as his country's foe was to be my enemy." (§§ 1, 2.)

The orator replies first to the charges of Antonius, which touch partly upon their personal relations to one another, partly on Cicero's previous political conduct.

With this he contrasts his own life and behaviour: "You, you it is who incited Caesar to all his deeds of violence against the state. . . . As trees and flowers arise from seeds, so were you the seed-corn of that calamitous war.

"You are mourning the slaughter of three armies of the Roman people. Antonius it was who slew them.

"You are regretting the loss of most eminent citizens :—Antonius bereft us of them too.

"The authority of the senate is abased. It is Antonius who has abased it. . . . As Helen was to the Trojans, so has he been to this city the cause of ruin and destruction." (§§ 53-55, in substance.)

"But let us quit the past. For this one day, this very day, the present moment at which I speak, justify yourself if you can. Why is the senate surrounded by a cordon of armed men? Why are your guardsmen listening to me sword in hand?

"Why are the doors of the temple of Concord not open? Why do you march into the forum your Ituraeans, the greatest barbarians in the world, with bow and arrow? He declares that he is doing this for his own protection. Is it not better a thousand times to perish than to be unable to live amongst one's fellow-citizens without the protection of men-at-arms?

"But believe me there is no protection in your method; it is with the love and goodwill of his countrymen, not with arms, that one should fence himself. The Roman people will tear away and wrest the arms from your hands, and, I pray, without hurt to us. But whatever your attitude to me and my party, you will not, believe me, while you follow such counsels as these, be able to maintain yourself for long. . . . . . The Roman people still knows to whom to commit the helm of state. . . . . Sweet is the name of peace, and wholesome the reality; but between peace and servitude, believe me, there is a great difference. Peace is the quiet enjoyment of freedom, servitude the uttermost of evils; to be averted at the cost not only of war, but even of death. And although our deliverers, Brutus and Cassius, have withdrawn from our view, yet they have left us the example of their deed. They have done what had never been done before. Tarquinius, who was king when kingship was still permitted at Rome, was assailed by Brutus in warfare only. Sp. Cassius, Sp. Maelius, M. Manlius were put to death simply because they were suspected of aspiring to kingly power. These, however, were the first who attacked sword in hand one who was no mere aspirant to kingship, but a reigning king. A deed which, glorious and divine as it is in itself, is also a clear example to imitate, particularly as the doers of it have attained a renown which the very heavens will scarcely contain. Although they won sufficient reward in the mere consciousness of their magnificent deed, still by a mortal immortality is not to be despised. Recall to your memory again, Antonius, the day on which you abolished the dictatorship; picture to your mind again the joy of the senate and people of Rome, and contrast with it this monstrous traffic and barter which you and your friends are conducting; and then you will see what a difference there is between praise and pelf. But in fact, just as persons when some malady has deadened the palate cannot relish the taste of food, so the profligate, covetous, and scandalous have no taste for true praise.

"But granted that praise cannot allure you to right conduct, cannot even fear deter you from the grossest misdeeds? You do not dread the courts of justice. If from conscious innocence, I commend you; if from the force that you wield, do you not perceive what the man has to fear who, like you, has no fear of the courts? But if you have no fear of brave and worthy citizens because you hold them aloof by force of arms, then, believe me, your creatures themselves will not much longer endure you. What a life it must be day and night to be in dread of your own friends! Unless, indeed, you hold yours attached by stronger obligations than he held some of his slayers, or are in any way comparable with him. He was gifted with intellect, understanding, memory, literary attainments, industry, reflection, vigilance. His exploits of war had been calamitous to the republic, but great nevertheless. For many years he had meditated reigning: and had, by great exertions and amid many dangers, accomplished his design. He had decoyed the thoughtless multitude by shows of games, public buildings, largesses, banquets: had bound to himself his friends by rewards, his adversaries by the show of clemency. In short, he had partly by fear, partly by tolerance, already induced upon a free state the habit of servitude. Only as regards the lust of power can I liken you to him; in all other things you are simply not to be compared with him. Fortunately, out of all the ills with which he has so deeply branded the country, this one good has resulted, that the Roman people has now learnt how far it may trust any man, to whom it may commit itself, against whom to be on its guard. Do you not think of these things, Antonius? nor understand that it is enough for men of spirit to have learnt that tyrannicide is intrinsically splendid, is a service that earns gratitude, a deed of glorious renown? Or think you that those who would not brook Caesar will brook you?

"Believe me, there will one day be an emulous rush to do the deed, no waiting for a tardy opportunity. I pray you, Antonius, even thus late to return to your sober senses: look at those from

whom you spring, not those with whom you
live: as for me, live on what terms with me
you will, but be reconciled to the republic. But
I leave you to consider your own future course: I
shall make avowal for myself alone. In my youth
I defended the republic: I will not forsake it in my
old age. I despised the daggers of Catilina: I shall
not shrink from yours. Yes, I would willingly offer up
my own person, if so be that by my death the freedom
of the state can be forthwith realized, so that the
travail of the Roman people may at length bring
forth that with which it has long been labouring.
For if in this very temple nigh twenty years ago I
declared that to one who has been consul death cannot come too early: with how much more truth can
I now declare the same thing of my old age! Yes,
conscript fathers, death is now to me even a thing
to wish for, now that I have accomplished my
full tale of honours and achievements. Two wishes
only do I cherish: one that, dying, I may leave
the Roman people free—and a greater boon the
gods could not award me; secondly, that each

may find such recompense as he shall deserve of the republic." (§§ 111-119.)

The young Octavianus had meantime entered the scene. His strained relations with Antonius determined even Cicero in his favour. "As far as I have been able to study him," he writes to Atticus (xv. 12), "he is a man of fair intelligence and spirit, and it seems as if he would be minded towards our 'heroes' as we wish; but how far we ought to trust his age, his name, his heirship, and his political schooling, will task our powers of deliberation." As soon as things had come to open enmity between Octavianus and Antonius, and Antonius had left Rome in order to wrest Hither Gaul from Decimus Brutus, Cicero returned to Rome, hoping, in reliance upon Octavianus, who was at the head of a considerable body of troops, to be able to establish anew the freedom of his country.

On the 20th of December, U.C. 710, B.C. 44, by means of his *Third Philippic* he brought the senate to a resolution that none of the governors then in provinces should leave them without permission of the senate, that Decimus Brutus should receive the commendation of the senate for his edict for the defence of his province against Antonius by force of arms; and lastly that the new consuls should as soon as possible report on the appointment of Octavianus as commander, and the rewarding of the troops for their services.

"The immortal gods," says he, "have given us these bulwarks; young Caesar for the city and Decimus Brutus for Gaul. . . . . Seize then the proffered opportunity, and remember this at last, that you, conscript fathers, are the leaders of the state, forming the most august assembly in the world.* Give the Roman people a proof that your counsel does not fail the state, seeing that Octavianus for his part declares that his valour shall not fail it.† My exhortation is not needed, for there is none so senseless as not to perceive that if we go to sleep over this crisis we shall

---

* Cp. Cineas' famous words to Pyrrhus, that the senate was an "assembly of kings."

† Or better, "Since they (the R. people) declare that their courage will not be found wanting."

have to bear a despotism not only cruel and tyrannical but disgraceful and outrageous. You know the insolence of Antonius, you know his friends, his household. To have to serve debauchees, roisterers, wanton and shameless men, gamblers and drunkards—this combines the keenest misery with the foulest disgrace.

"If, however—which heaven forfend!—the last hour of the republic has arrived, let us, the foremost men in all the world, imitate the example of noble gladiators, who fall to the ground with honour. Let us fall with dignity rather than serve with disgrace." (§§ 34, 35.)

In the *Fourth Philippic*,* delivered on the same day, he communicated to the people the resolutions of the senate, and after the people had expressed approval of all, he thus concluded his speech:

"As generals are wont, after forming order of battle, to exhort their troops, however ready they may see their men to be for the combat, so will I do. Aglow and alive as you are with enthusiasm for the recovery

---

* Its genuineness has been unsuccessfully attacked: *v.* Mr. King's Introd.

of your freedom, I will encourage you further. The struggle in which you are engaged is not with an enemy with whom any terms of peace are possible, for no longer as before does he thirst for your liberties; in his rage he longs for your life-blood. He deems no sport so sweet as butchery and carnage, as the slaughter of citizens before his eyes. You have to do not with a guilt-stained and impious man, but with a monstrous and horrible wild beast. Now that he is fallen into a pit he must be crushed in it, for if he once escapes there will be no shunning his vengeance, however barbarous. He is now held in check, pinned down, and menaced by the troops which we already have, and soon will be also by those which the new consuls will in a few days arm. Let not your present zeal grow cold, Quirites. Never in any cause has your unanimity been so great; never were you so heartily in accord with the senate. And no wonder, for the question is not on what conditions we are to live, but whether we are to live at all or perish in torments and ignominy. It is true that nature has subjected all men to the prospect of death, yet valour have to bear a despotism not only cruel and tyrannical but disgraceful and outrageous. You know the insolence of Antonius, you know his friends, his household. To have to serve debauchees, roisterers, wanton and shameless men, gamblers and drunkards—this combines the keenest misery with the foulest disgrace.

"If, however—which heaven forfend!—the last hour of the republic has arrived, let us, the foremost men in all the world, imitate the example of noble gladiators, who fall to the ground with honour. Let us fall with dignity rather than serve with disgrace." (§§ 34, 35.)

In the *Fourth Philippic*,* delivered on the same day, he communicated to the people the resolutions of the senate, and after the people had expressed approval of all, he thus concluded his speech:

"As generals are wont, after forming order of battle, to exhort their troops, however ready they may see their men to be for the combat, so will I do. Aglow and alive as you are with enthusiasm for the recovery

---

* Its genuineness has been unsuccessfully attacked: *v.* Mr. King's Introd.

of your freedom, I will encourage you further. The struggle in which you are engaged is not with an enemy with whom any terms of peace are possible, for no longer as before does he thirst for your liberties; in his rage he longs for your life-blood. He deems no sport so sweet as butchery and carnage, as the slaughter of citizens before his eyes. You have to do not with a guilt-stained and impious man, but with a monstrous and horrible wild beast. Now that he is fallen into a pit he must be crushed in it, for if he once escapes there will be no shunning his vengeance, however barbarous. He is now held in check, pinned down, and menaced by the troops which we already have, and soon will be also by those which the new consuls will in a few days arm. Let not your present zeal grow cold, Quirites. Never in any cause has your unanimity been so great; never were you so heartily in accord with the senate. And no wonder, for the question is not on what conditions we are to live, but whether we are to live at all or perish in torments and ignominy. It is true that nature has subjected all men to the prospect of death, yet valour will generally avert a grievous and ignoble death, and valour is the peculiar virtue of the Roman race and stock. Keep this fast, Quirites, for your forefathers left it you as an inheritance.

"All else is deceptive, uncertain, transitory, changeable. Valour alone strikes root so firm and deep that it can never be shaken by any force whatever, nor dislodged from its ground.

"By it your forefathers first conquered the whole of Italy, then razed Carthage, overthrew Numantia, reduced beneath their sway the mightiest kings, the most warlike nations.

"Your forefathers, it is true, had to deal with a foe who possessed a state, a senate-house, a treasury, citizens who were at one in their action and sentiments, some reasonable basis, if circumstances required it, for peace and amnesty.

"But this present foe of yours beleaguers your state, but himself has none. The senate, that is, the great council of the world, he longs to abolish; public council of his own he has none. Your treasury he has drained: treasury of his own he has not. How can he possess the general accord of citizens at a time when he has no city at all? What basis of peace again is possible with one who is cruel beyond conception, and utterly faithless? In fact, Quirites, the Roman people, the conqueror of all nations, has before it a conflict with none other than an assassin, a brigand, a Spartacus. For as to his habit of priding himself on his resemblance to Catilina, it is true he resembles him in wickedness, but in energy he is quite inferior. Catilina, having no army, worked one up straightway: Antonius took over an army only to lose it. As the power of Catilina, however, by my vigilance, by the authoritative action of the senate, by your zeal and bravery, was shattered, so you will shortly hear that the shameful robber-warfare of Antonius has by your unprecedented accord with the senate, by the fortune and bravery of your armies and leaders, been overpowered. For my part, I will, to the utmost reach of my power, by care and pains, by nightly vigilance, by dint of my influence and my counsels, spare no effort that in my opinion can further your freedom: it would be a crime for me to act otherwise, considering the high honours which your bounty has bestowed on me." (§§ 11-16.)

<small>U.C. 711, B.C. 43.
Fifth and remaining Philippics.</small>

On the 1st of January of the next year, U.C. 711, B.C. 43, Cicero, in his *Fifth Philippic* pressed for a declaration of war against Antonius, who was besieging Decimus Brutus in Mutina.

The senate was inclined towards his motion; three days afterwards, however, the proposal of certain prevailed, to send envoys to Antonius first, and by them to charge him to raise the siege and submit to the authority of the senate. These resolutions Cicero communicated to the people on the same day, January 4th, in his *Sixth Philippic*, and exhorted them by their steadfastness to strengthen the senate in its previous resolve. " That Rome should be enslaved—the thought is impious—the people whom the immortal gods have willed should command all nations. Matters have reached the crisis. Your liberty is staked on the combat. Either you must conquer—and with your patriotism and your unanimity, **conquer you will**—or else **accept** anything rather than slavery. Other nations may endure that: liberty **is** the inalienable possession **of the Roman people!**" (§ 19.)

The envoys who had been **sent** meantime, lingered over their return. **Once** more, at the end of January, Cicero, in the *Seventh Philippic*, counselled the senate **to break off** all negotiations with Antonius. " I, who like all loyal men (and yet more than they all), have ever set my heart on peace, especially internal **peace** **—for** my whole active career has spent itself in the forum, in the senate-house, in averting the perils of my friends: from this I have attained the highest offices, from this my modest fortune and whatever measure of repute belongs to me—I, too, nursling of peace that I am, who (not to be presumptuous) should not have become even what little I am, but for internal peace, I hazard that word of danger— though I tremble **to** think **how** you will take it, senators—but in consideration of my continuous anxiety to uphold and promote the honour of your order, I beg and implore you, although it prove an unpalatable or incredible utterance on Marcus Cicero's part, to listen without offence to what I shall say, and not to reject it until I have explained its purport—it is I, the invariable advocate (I will repeat it), and invariable adviser of peace, who now refuse a peace with M. Antonius! . . . And why will I have no peace? Because it is base, perilous, impossible!" (§§ 7-9)

After the interruption of negotiations at the beginning of February, war was resolved upon, but it was to be designated not as *war* but as a civil rising (*tumultus*) only. Cicero, in his *Eighth Philippic*, repudiates this half-heartedness. "What is the matter in dispute? Some persons did not wish the term 'war' to be used in the resolution, but would rather have it styled a rising. These people showed their ignorance both of realities and even of words.

"A war without a rising is possible, a rising without war is impossible.

" Our ancestors therefore spoke of an Italian rising, because it was internal, and of a Gallic rising, because it broke out on the borders of Italy; otherwise they never used the word. That a rising is a more serious matter than a war may be inferred from the fact that exemptions from service are valid in a war, but not in a rising. Hence it results, as I have stated, that a war may exist without a rising, but no rising without war.

"And indeed, as now there is no middle course between peace and war, a rising, if it is not war, must necessarily mean peace; could any statement or idea be more absurd?" (§§ 3, 4.)

Of the envoys sent to Antonius by the senate, Ser. Sulpicius Rufus had scarcely reached his destination when he died.

In the *Ninth Philippic* Cicero proposed in the senate public honours to his memory, and at the same time renewed his attacks on Antonius.

In the *Tenth Philippic* Cicero procured from the senate a formal sanction of the measures taken by M. Brutus in Macedonia and Illyria on his own responsibility.

Brutus had made himself master of Macedonia, Illyria, and Greece, had attracted to his cause the troops stationed in these countries, and had driven Caius, the brother of Marcus Antonius, out of the province of Macedonia assigned to him by the latter, and had shut him up in Apollonia. Cassius too had refused to Dolabella, Antonius' colleague in the consulate, the province of Syria assigned to him.

In the *Eleventh Philippic** Cicero lays before the senate a proposal to approve the acts of Cassius also, and to declare Dolabella a public enemy for having attacked Trebonius, governor of Asia, and cruelly put him to death.

In the *Twelfth Philippic* Cicero repels the renewed proposals of Piso and Calenus to send envoys to Antonius to treat for peace. The *Thirteenth Philippic* † is directed against Lepidus, who likewise urged peace.

Cicero finally delivered the *Fourteenth Philippic* ‡ on the arrival of the news of the victory of the consuls Hortius and Pansa over Antonius at Forum Gallorum. He proposed therein a fifty-days' thanksgiving for the

---

* Middle of March, B.C. 43.
† March 20, B.C. 43.
‡ April 22, B.C. 43.

victory, the title of Imperator for the consuls and Octavianus, decorations and rewards for the soldiers, and the outlawry of Antonius and his adherents.

Cicero expiated his enmity against Antonius by his death, after the latter had formed a coalition with Octavianus and Lepidus, the three dividing the supreme power among them, under the title of *Triumviri reipublicae constituendae*. He was proscribed on the proposal of Antonius, and in course of flight was overtaken near Caieta by the military tribune Popilius Laenas, and slain by the centurion Herennius, December 7th, U.C. 711, B.C. 43. His head and his right hand were exposed upon the Rostra.

<small>U.C. 711, B.C. 43. December 7th, Death of Cicero.</small>

CHAPTER III.

Ancient opinions of Cicero and his oratory—His wit—Contemporary orators—His letters.

ASINIUS POLLIO, Cicero's contemporary, thus pronounces upon his character (quoted by Seneca, Suas. vi. 24): "It would be superfluous, amidst so many works that will remain for all time, to eulogize the genius and the writings of this great man. He was favoured alike by nature and fortune. He retained until old age an attractive presence and sound health. A long peace too, in the arts of which he was well versed, stood him in good stead. For the judicial procedure being still carried on with antique severity, there was a large body of accused persons, most of whom he attached to himself by his forensic services in procuring their acquittal.

"Fortune was further in his favour when he stood for the consulship, and in the conduct of his high offices under the good-will and assistance of providence. Had he but known how to support good-fortune with more moderation and ill-fortune with more courage! For as often as he encountered either one or the other he deemed no change possible. Hence it was that many violent storms of ill-will broke upon him, and his enemies could with the more confidence attack him, since he challenged enmities with more courage than he could maintain them. But since perfect virtue has never been the portion of a mortal, a man must be judged according to what is most prominent in his life and character. I should not myself deem his end pitiable, had he not thought death so wretched."

To the same effect the historian Livy (quoted in Seneca, Suas. vi. 22) : " He bore none of all his reverses as a man should, except his death, and this upon a sound judgment might appear less hard, since he suffered no greater cruelty at the hands of his victorious enemies than he himself, if the same fortune had favoured him, would have inflicted. But if his faults be set against his virtues, he still remains a noble, great, and famous man, who could only have received his due of praise if there had been a Cicero to pronounce it."

The Emperor Augustus once entered the chamber of one of his grandchildren, who had in hand and was reading one of Cicero's writings, but, seeing his grandfather, was frightened and hid the book. Augustus however, noticing this, took the book, read in it for a long time, and gave it him back with the words: Λόγιος ἀνήρ, ὦ παῖ, λόγιος καὶ φιλόπατρις—"A learned man, my child, learned and patriotic!" (Plutarch, *Vit. Cic.* xlix.)

Amongst the writings of Cicero his speeches hold indisputably the first rank. They are mostly taken down as he delivered them: some of them were worked up by him later, and others were never delivered at all. The number of his speeches is considerable: he himself says (*Orat.* §§ 108): "No orator, not even a Greek, with his greater leisure, has written so many and such multifarious speeches as I." We know the titles of more than a hundred speeches; of these fifty-eight* are preserved more or less complete. We possess fragments of about twenty others.

The *Pridie quam in exilium iret* and *Responsio ad orationem invectivam Sallustii* are school exercises of a later date foisted upon Cicero.

For five speeches we still possess remains of the valuable commentaries of the learned Q. Asconius Pedianus, who died U.C. 842, A.D. 88, in the 85th year of his age. These are grounded on a thorough study of original authorities. The orations are divided into forensic (*forenses: in causa privata, in causa publica*) and political (*in senatu, pro contione ad Quirites*).

They differ in interest and value. The political speeches and those *in causa publica* afforded the orator worthier subject-matter and of a higher order, and more opportunity for displaying his brilliant talent, than the private orations. The composer of the dialogue *De Oratoribus* (37) rightly says on this point: "It is not the speeches which Demosthenes composed against his guardians that

---

* 57 (Teuffel).

have made him famous, nor the defences of P. Quinctius and Licinius Archias that have made Cicero a great orator; but Catilina, Milo, Verres, and Antonius have invested him with his renown." The same writer has thus descanted on the difference between Cicero's earlier and his later speeches: "In nothing does Cicero so much surpass the orators of his time as in the judiciousness of his method.

"He was the first carefully to finish a speech, to practise a choice of diction, to bestow skill upon the composition. He then endeavoured to make some passages specially attractive, and has struck out novel thoughts, particularly in those speeches which he composed in ripe age towards the end of his life, that is after he had himself made progress, and had learnt by practice and experiment what speaking of the highest order was.

"For his earlier speeches are not free from the faults of the older time. He drags in his openings, is prolix in his narratives, lingers towards the close. He is slowly roused, he seldom breaks out in fire, few of his periods have a graceful and lustrous close.

One can cull nothing from him, quote nothing; and as in a rough building the walls are firm, it may be, and durable, but without polish or brilliancy. I, however, would have an orator, like a householder of wealth and splendour, inhabit a house that not only affords shelter against rain and storm, but that shall also gladden the eyes that regard it, and that is not only provided with such household stuff as is indispensable, but can also show gold and precious stones among its garniture, which if we will we may often handle and admire.

"Some things must be put away because now worn out and musty: no word should be used which has become rusty; no sentence allowed which is formed in the dragging and inartistic fashion of the annalists.

"Further, one must avoid offensive and tasteless buffoonery, must vary the structure of his phrases, and not conclude all the clauses in one unvarying manner. I refuse to laugh at the 'wheel of fortune,'* 'Verrine justice = pork-broth' † and the expression

---

* "rota fortunae," in Pison. 10.
† ius tam nequam Verrinum (Verr. i. 16).

which appears at almost every third sentence in the speeches, "would seem to be the case," for even this I only reluctantly refer to, and there is more which I altogether pass over, and yet this kind of thing alone do those admire and imitate who call themselves orators of the old stamp." (*Dial. de Oratoribus*, 22.)

Whatever measure of truth this judgment contains, the taste of the time and the personal prepossession of the writer had exercised some influence on it.

Quintilian (xii., 1, 19) unconditionally styles Cicero the best orator, not indeed in an ideal sense, but according to the usual acceptation, in which the best is he who is surpassed by no other.

Cicero's personality contributed much to the effect of his speeches. He himself avows that when he spoke it was not the strength of talent, but of feeling which fired him. (*Nulla me ingenii, sed magna vis animi inflammat.*) Cicero puts into his brother's mouth a description of his inspiration in speaking (*De Divinatione* 1 § 80): "Democritus says that without ecstasy no poet can be great, and Plato maintains the same opinion. . . . . Again, can your oratory in the law-court, can your delivery itself express stormy vehemence, serious repose, the most manifold moods, unless the heart itself is more or less moved? I, at least, have often observed in yourself, and, to pass to a less serious profession, in your friend the actor Aesopus, such a glow in the countenance and gestures that a kind of inspiration appeared to have transported you out of your senses."

On the other hand Cicero understood how to give piquancy to his speeches by wit and satire. His wit was known and dreaded; he employed it in ordinary life as well as in his speeches.*

Even in his lifetime Trebonius arranged a collection of his witticisms, and sent the book to Cicero; who, writing to him on the subject (*ad Fam.* xv. 21), says, " What a strong declaration of your affection is the book you have sent me! first, in that every one of my utterances appears witty to you, which perhaps with

---

* Thus Quint. vi. 3.3 who calls him "nimius risus affectator." Cluent. ch. xxvi. is a favourable example. "What a witty consul we have," said Cato as Cic. in his *pro Murena* held up his Stoicism to ridicule, Plut. Dem. et Cic. i. His 'false wit' is criticised, *Spectator*, No. 61.

others might not have been the case ; and then because those utterances, be they witty or otherwise, when you retail them, acquire the highest charm." Caesar, too, admitted them with a special predilection into his collection of witty ana*, and had so fine an ear for Ciceronian wit, that he at once detected spurious sayings as such (*ad Fam.* ix. 16).

After Cicero's death his freedman Tiro issued a complete collection in three books†. Macrobius has also preserved us some of his witty anecdotes. (*Sat.* II. 2.3).

Quintilian (vi. 3) expresses himself thus about Cicero's propensity to witty raillery, which was often made matter of reproach to him. "The opinion has been held that Cicero not only outside the law-courts but also in his speeches strained too much after the ludicrous. To me, however—be it that I judge him partially or that I suffer from an intemperate affection for one so superlative in oratory—it seems that he possessed‡ a strange charm of polished wit, for he used

---

* ἀποφθέγματα.
† Quint. vi. 3.5.
‡ mira quaedam urbanitas.

frequently in ordinary conversation, as well as in forensic debate and in the examination of witnesses, to say more witty things than anyone else. . . . It might have been wished that his freedman, Tiro, or whoever it was that issued the three books on this subject, had restricted himself in the number of his witty anecdotes, and had shown more judgment in their selection than diligence in their compilation. He would then have furnished less material to Cicero's traducers, who in this, as in their criticism of his genius generally, will always more easily find some flaw to remove than some improvement to make."

Cicero himself (*ad Fam.* ix. 16) owns: "If I would avoid the character which some of my trenchant and humorous expressions earn me I must renounce the character of a man of parts. If I could do this I would not refuse to do it." In a letter to Volumnius (*ad Fam.* vii. 32) he complains of the spurious witticisms which were current under his name, and at the same time gives him the tests by which he was to distinguish the spurious from the genuine. He might stake his chance in a trial on the certainty that a witticism was not of his authorship if there were no raciness in the equivoque, if the exaggeration were tasteless, if the verbal play did not tell, if the jest did not startle, if all that remained were not of the kind required by him in the second book of his treatise on the Orator.

As regards Cicero's relation to the Greek orators, he recognised them as his masters and models, though not conceiving them yet to have reached the ideal of the art:—

"Far from my admiring my own works, so severe and exacting is my standard that Demosthenes himself does not satisfy my requirements. Although he surpasses every rival in oratory of every kind, nevertheless he does not always content my ear, so exacting and insatiate is it, and so much does it crave for something transcending the commonplace. . .
He attains much, while I attempt much. He has the power, I the will to speak as every occasion requires. He is great, for great orators preceded him and were his contemporaries. I, too, might have done

something great if I had been able to attain the goal of my efforts in a city in which, as Antonius says, no real orator had ever been heard before." (*Orator* §§ 104, 105.)

The verdict preserved by Jerome (*Epist.* 52 *ad Nepotian.*) is much to the point : " Demosthenes has wrested from you, Cicero, the honour of being the first orator ; you from him that of being the only one." (*Demosthenes tibi praeripuit, ne esses primus orator, tu illi ne solus.*)

It throws a fine light upon Cicero's character that he was always upon the most honourable terms with the orators of his own time who, side by side with him, strove in the same domain for renown and distinction. He was as far from envy and jealousy as from presumption and the assertion of his superiority.

Even those who, like Calvus,* were his opponents he criticised without malice, fairly and charitably. The man with whom at the very outset of his oratorical career he contended for precedence was Hortensius.

---

* C. Licinius Macer Calvus, *v.* infra.

Q. Hortensius Hortalus, born U.C. 640, B.C. 114, an aristocrat alike in his politics and his way of life, a man of brilliant talent, dominated the rostra for a certain time, by an eloquence formed after the Asiatic orators, grandiloquent, supported by an excellent memory and a lively and artistic delivery, suited rather to the actor than to the orator. (*Cic. Brut.* §§ 301-303.) He was fond of expatiating upon commonplaces (*Quint.* ii., 1), and distinguished himself from other orators by a precise statement of the division, and a summary recapitulation of what he himself had said, and what had been advanced against him. He was animated by an almost passionate zeal for oratory.

He never let a day pass without either speaking in the forum, or practising elsewhere, very often doing both in the same day (*Brut. ib.*). After his consulate, however, U.C. 685, B C. 69, he abated in his zeal; he gave himself up to the enjoyment of life, the brilliancy of his oratory continually declined (*Brut.* § 320), and Cicero soon succeeded to the position which until now Hortensius had held in the forum. He died U.C. 704,

B.C. 50, and Cicero erected a noble monument to him in the introduction to his *Brutus*. "I was grieved," says he, "because I had lost, not as most people thought, an opponent and disparager of my distinction, but a comrade and associate in glorious endeavour. And indeed, if in a lower field of art, famous poets, as is related, have ere now mourned the death of a contemporary poet, with what feelings was I bound to bear the decease of one with whom it was more glorious to wage combat than to have no antagonist at all? especially as we never hindered one the other in our career, but, on the contrary, advanced each other by mutual service, suggestion, and admiration." (*Brut.* §§ 2, 3.)

Of the orations of Hortensius there are not any fragments extant. Other contemporary orators were in part pupils of Cicero. To these belongs M. Caelius Rufus, born U.C. 672, B.C. 82, who was brought to Cicero by his father. He was a young man of much talent, but a somewhat dissolute course of life, as Cicero himself was obliged to admit in his speech in his defence. He met a violent death at Thurii, U.C. 706,

B.C. 48, in the commotions excited by him in company with Milo (*Caesar B. Civ.*, iii., 22).

A collection of letters from Caelius to Cicero is contained in the eighth book of the *Epistulae ad Familiares*. Cicero (*Brut.* § 273) characterises him as a brilliant and elevated, at the same time witty and refined orator, whose forte lay in public speeches and in prosecutions. In like terms Quintilian (x. 1, 115) pronounces upon him:—

"Caelius possessed much talent, and displays, especially in his speeches as prosecutor, much refinement; it might have been wished that a more virtuous disposition as well as a longer life had fallen to his lot." Seneca (*de ira*, iii., 8) calls him most wrathful of orators (*oratorem iracundissimum*).*

M. Junius Brutus (born U.C. 668, B.C. 86, died U.C. 712, B.C. 42), a close friend of Cicero's, followed nevertheless, in oratory as in philosophy, his own course.

He distinguished himself in his writings, as in his

---

* Dining with a client who kept studiously assenting to whatever he said, he broke out at last, "dic aliquid contra, ut duo simus." *Ibid.*

life, by earnestness and severity. "In his philosophical writings M. Brutus excels, far more so than in his speeches. You can tell that what he says comes from the heart." (Quint. x. 1, 123.) C. Julius Caesar also stands out as an original orator. Quintilian criticises him in the following terms (x. 1, 114): "If Caesar had devoted himself solely to the forum, he would have been the only one of our orators worthy to be named with Cicero. He possesses such force, such keenness, such passion, that the same spirit is apparent in his speeches as in his wars." In the *Brutus* (§ 252), Cicero puts into the mouth of Atticus the following words: "My judgment of Caesar is that of almost all orators he speaks the choicest Latin."

The famous jurist, Servius Sulpicius Rufus (U.C. 649, B.C. 105—U.C. 711, B.C. 43), shone less as an orator. Cicero awarded him in this field but moderate praise (*Brutus* § 155). "By three orations," says Quintilian (x. 1, 115), "he won for himself a not undeserved name." We still possess of his a letter of condolence addressed to Cicero on the loss of his daughter Tullia (*ad Fam.* iv. 5). The brief and unquiet life of C. Scribonius Curio hindered the development of his talent, which Cicero rates very highly.* He met his end in the civil war in Africa, U.C. 705, B.C. 49. Cicero praises M. Calidius for his carefulness in details, the suavity, repose, and perspicuity of his speeches, but censures the phlegmatic character of his delivery.† In opposition to Cicero stood Caius Licinius Macer Calvus (U.C. 672-706, B.C. 82-48), who figured also as a poet, son of the annalist Licinius Macer. "For a long time he carried on a very bitter struggle with Cicero for precedence in oratory," says the rhetorician Seneca (*Controv.* vii. 19).‡ Different

---

* *Brut.* § 280.

† *Brut.* §§ 274 276.

‡ The New Attic School of oratory, so called, set up the genuine Attic orators, Lysias and Demosthenes, as its models, in place of the Rhodian and the still more turgid Asiatic masters of eloquence. According to Mommsen, who sees in "Ciceronianism" a sort of mysterious infatuation with which the human race is periodically visited, the "strange idolatry" of graceful language empty of thought, this younger school represents a revolt against the Ciceronian manner. Brutus, Caelius, Calvus, Curio, Calidius, Pollio, all belonged to it. *V.* Momms. iv. ii. 611.

verdicts were pronounced upon him even in ancient times. "I have found people," says Quintilian (x. i. 115), "who preferred Calvus to everyone. Others, again, who deemed with Cicero* that he wasted vital energy upon excessive self-depreciation. Still his language is pure, earnest, chastened, and often highly impassioned as well." According to Seneca (*l. c.*), he lacks repose and serenity; everywhere there is an excited and restless touch. His principal fault was that he sought in a one-sided and exaggerated way to imitate Attic simplicity, as Cicero repeatedly insists, while he always does justice to his talents, his culture, and the conscientiousness of his aim.

As he said of Curio, so he does of him, that he would have attained great renown in oratory if he had lived long enough. (*Brutus*, ch. lxxxi.)

C. Asinius Pollio appears as Cicero's most important opponent. He again reflects the old Roman orators, and in his own speeches was careful it is true, but stiff and cold.

---

* *Brut.* § 283.

He made his first appearance (U.C. 700, B.C. 54) in a prosecution of Caius Cato.* His literary and critical activity reached its climax in the period after Cicero. Calvus and Asinius drew with them others also who, in their preference for Attic simplicity and old Roman uniformity, pronounced a condemnatory verdict against Cicero.

"It has for some time been known," so runs the dialogue *de Oratoribus* (18), "that even Cicero did not lack his detractors, to whom he seemed high-flown, bombastic, not sufficiently concise, in fact unduly luxuriant, over-exuberant, and not Attic enough." The same dialogue (25) gives a short, pertinent characterisation of all the orators who grouped themselves around Cicero: "Calvus has greater conciseness, Asinius a more rhythmic cadence, Caesar more brilliancy, Caelius more bitterness, Brutus more earnestness, Cicero more passion, fulness, and force. Still all bear the hall-mark of a sound eloquence, so that if one takes up all their writings at the same

---

* Tac. dial. de or. 34.

time, amid all their diversity of intellect a resemblance and relationship of method and endeavour is recognisable."

Cicero's Letters:
Epp. ad Fam. xvi., ad Att. xvi., ad Q. fratrem iii., ad Brutum ii. : ad Octavianum.

Even more than the Speeches the Letters of Cicero are a faithful record of his sentiments and aspirations, and are likewise most important documents for his own history and that of his time. Cicero himself appears in his life to have actually made preparations for a collection.

He wrote to Atticus (xvi. 5) : "There is no collection of my letters, but Tiro has about seventy, and some of my letters must be obtained from you for the purpose. It is true I must first of all revise and correct them ; till then they must not be published." We now possess a threefold collection, drawn up, it is said, by Tiro after Cicero's death. The first group, the so-called *Epistulae ad Familiares*, comprises sixteen books of letters to sundry persons. The letters belong to the period U.C. 691-711 (B.C. 63-43). They are not arranged in chronological order, but pretty much according to the persons to whom they were addressed. Beside Cicero's letters, those of other persons to which these relate are often given. Book VIII. contains only the correspondence of Caelius with Cicero. Book XIV. is a collection of Cicero's family letters to his wife Terentia and his children. Book XV., 1, 2, give statements to the government about the events in Cilicia during Cicero's proconsulate. Book XVI. contains Cicero's letters to his freedman and friend Tiro.

The letters are very various in subject and form. Cicero himself, writing to C. Curio (*ad Fam.* ii. 4), expresses himself respecting the different species of letters: "You are well aware that there are many sorts of letters, of which the most unmistakable—this being, in fact, the very purpose for which letters were invented—is when we inform those at a distance of anything which our interest or theirs requires that they should know. Letters of this kind you certainly cannot expect from me, for there are certainly those among your dependants who will inform you of your own affairs either personally or in writing. About my own affairs there is nothing new to communicate. Besides this kind of letter there are also two others, in which it is a great pleasure to me to engage, one the lively and confidential, the other the grave and serious.

"Which of these two least becomes me now I cannot decide. Am I to write to you in the merry vein? Upon my honour I do not think a true citizen is to be found who can jest in times like these. Or am I to write to you of grave and important affairs? Could Cicero write to Curio seriously at all without writing about the state? But on that matter it stands with me thus: I do not dare* to write what I really think, or care to write what I do not think." The collection affords examples of all these three kinds. Those letters which deal with political matters, especially those in which Cicero himself took part, are written with special reflection and care, evidently because they were even at the time designed for publicity.

---

* Reading *audeam* with Tyrrell.

In the confidential letters to his friends and relatives he delivers himself more unreservedly.

The second collection, the sixteen books of letters to Atticus (*Epistularum ad Atticum libri xvi.*), are chronologically* arranged. The first eleven letters of the first book are dated before his consulate, U.C. 686-691, B.C. 68-63; the remainder U.C. 692-710, B.C. 62-44. Some letters to other people beside Atticus are interspersed.

On this collection Cornelius Nepos (*Vit. Att.* 16) observes: "Cicero loved Atticus so well that even his own brother Quintus was not dearer to him or more intimate with him.

"Beside the writings which he published, in which he mentions Atticus, the sixteen volumes of letters which he wrote to him from the time of his consulate until the end of his life witness to the fact. He who reads these will not particularly lack a coherent history of the times.

"For all connected with the aims of political chiefs,

---

* Particular letters are sometimes misplaced.

the mistakes of leaders, the changes in the state is so amply described that everything appears in the clearest light, and we readily come to believe that their wisdom is a sort of second-sight.

"For Cicero had not only predicted what happened in his own life, but has prophet-like announced what is now coming to pass." The letters not only contain political intelligence, but also treat of personal and domestic occurrences, literary subjects, and the like. The language is less elaborated : to his confidential friend, the writer opens himself out : Greek words and forms of speech and quotations from Greek authors are interspersed very freely.

Many circumstances, which were known to his friend, are only obscurely hinted at. It may be in general remarked of these letters that, not being intended for publicity, they are spontaneous outpourings of the heart to a friend.

The third collection is formed of the three books of letters to Quintus Cicero (*Epistularum ad Quintum fratrem libri iii.*).

The first letter of Book I. is an admirable exposition to his brother of the main points to be observed in general in the administration of a province, and of that which was expected in particular of him. Quintus at this time had been for two years in charge as propraetor of the province of Asia, and his administration had against his own wishes been continued for another year.

The other letters touch partly on political, partly on domestic occurrences, or treat of mutual studies and fresh productions in the field of literature.

The genuineness of a fourth collection of letters to and from Marcus Brutus in two books, written entirely after Caesar's death, has been called in question.*

The letter to Octavianus, which goes under Cicero's name, is certainly spurious. Other collections, those to Cornelius Nepos, to Caesar, to Pompeius, to Hirtius and others, are lost.

---

* Professor Tyrrell accepts them: *v.* his ed. of the Letters, p. lxii.

CHAPTER IV.

Cicero's Rhetorical Treatises.

De inventione ii. :
De oratore iii. :
Brutus : Orator.

CICERO was not only a practical orator, but has also the merit of having first, after sundry imperfect attempts of predecessors, created a complete system of Roman rhetoric. Well acquainted as he was with the Greek rhetoricians, while he made use of them, he undertook an independent task : drawing upon his own experience, and having in view the needs of the Roman orator, to teach his countrymen the art of eloquence in a series of treatises.

He had already as a youth made his first essay, compiling from extracts and notes taken from the Greek rhetoricians, particularly Hermagoras, and with the assistance of the treatise *Ad Herennium*, a Rhetoric which, however, remained unfinished. These are the two books *Rhetorica*, or as they are generally styled from the topic discussed in them, the *De inventione*. Cicero afterwards himself regarded this as an imperfect youthful work, which after he had acquired greater experience by constant practice in public speaking, he felt bound to surpass by a more solid performance.*

This was done in the treatise Upon the Orator (*De oratore, libri iii*.) which he dedicated to his brother Quintus; composed U.C. 699, B.C. 55, during the time when the turmoil in the state raised by the ambition of Pompeius and Crassus hampered his political activity, when, as he writes to Lentulus (*ad Fam*. i. 9), he had almost entirely renounced oratory, and returned again to the gentler muses (*ad mansuetiores musas*).

He himself (*ad Att.* xiii. 19) declares that he finds in this treatise a peculiar delight, and it does in fact recommend itself by the remarkable carefulness of its execution, and by its luxuriant and polished

---

* De orat. i. § 5.

diction.* The model present to his view was Aristotle's Rhetoric : whilst, however, he follows him in fundamental principles, resting the definition of the orator in the fact that by working on the understanding, the imagination, and the feelings of his hearers he brings them over to his view,† nevertheless in the execution of his design he is thoroughly original. The dryness of a systematic presentation of the subject is relieved by the dialogue form.

It is true that this is not carried out by the method of the Platonic Socrates in which the final result is gradually attained by a process of questions and answers ; but the chief personages handle the thesis assigned to each according to his own characteristics in a connected speech, whilst the secondary characters only contribute to the continuation of the discussion by their questions and incidental remarks. The

---

* " The most finished perhaps of Cicero's compositions. An air of grandeur and magnificence reigns throughout. The characters of the aged senators are finely conceived, and the whole company is invested with an almost religious majesty." (J. H. Newman, quoted by Dr. Sandys, *Orator*, introd. xlix.)

† Persuadere docendo, conciliando, movendo.

investiture of the theme in dialogue form rests on a supposed narration which Cicero had had from the mouth of Cotta, who was present at the conversation. Crassus in the last year of his life (U C. 663, B.C. 91), not long before his death, had during the festivities of the *ludi Romani* retired to his country seat at Tusculum in order to recruit after the struggles in which he had to engage in the senate with the consul Philippus. Here came Scaevola the augur, his father-in-law, and Antonius, his friend and political associate. Two young men, C. Cotta, who was already a candidate for the tribuneship, and P. Sulpicius, accompanied Crassus to the country at the same time.

On the first day they conversed about the sad crisis of the state, and after that cheered themselves over the social meal. On the following day, as they were strolling about in the open air, Scaevola, in imitation of Socrates in the Phaedrus of Plato, invited them to seat themselves under a shady plane-tree and so enjoy their morning's talk. It so chanced that Crassus began the conversation, and praised

Cotta and Sulpicius for their zeal in oratory, in which they not only surpassed their contemporaries, but might even compare favourably in faculty with their elders. "For," says he (§ 30), "nothing appears to me a more excellent gift than to be able by speech to hold assemblies in your grasp, to fascinate their attention, to sway their will at pleasure towards a thing or from it. That is the one thing which in every free nation, and above all in states which enjoy peace and repose, has always flourished best and attained supremacy.

"For what is so wonderful as that out of an innumerable crowd of men one comes forward who stands alone, or almost alone, in having the power to exercise a faculty which nature has bestowed upon all?

"Or what is so delightful to hear and witness as a speech graced and resplendent with wise thoughts and weighty words? or so powerful and grand as when the passion of the people, the scruples of the judges, the conservatism of the senate, is overborne by the speech of one man? What again is so kingly, so noble, so beneficent, as to render help to suppliants, to cheer the dejected, to bring men rescue, to deliver them from perils, to preserve them to their country? What, on the other hand, so necessary as always to have weapons with which to protect yourself, to challenge the unprincipled, or to avenge provocation? Further, not to dwell continually on the forum, with its court of justice, rostra, and senate-house, what can be a more delightful recreation in leisure, or better befits a cultured man than brilliant and refined conversation?

"The one thing which constitutes our superiority to the brutes is that we can converse with one another, can communicate our thoughts by speech.

"Why then should not a man rightly admire this, and think himself bound to apply all diligence to distinguish himself amongst his kind by this faculty, even as by it especially he surpasses the brutes? But the chief consideration remains: what other power has availed to unite scattered men at one centre, has transferred them from savagery and barbarism to our present civilisation as men and citizens, or in states already constituted has been able to sketch out laws, rights, and tribunals? But, not to expatiate further on a limitless theme, I will thus briefly sum up my opinion:—On the wise guidance of a finished orator depends not only his own dignity, but also very largely the wellbeing of a great number of individuals as well as of the state in its entirety.

"Continue then, my young friends, your exertions, and carry on those studies to which you have devoted yourselves, so as to bring honour to yourselves, profit to your friends and advantage to the state."

Scaevola hereupon takes up the conversation, approving in general terms the utterance of Crassus in praise of eloquence, but combating what he had laid down about the salutary influence of orators upon the founding and maintenance of states; orators, said he, had often proved the occasion rather of the fall of states. He also denies the necessity of such a comprehensive knowledge as Crassus requires of orators: it is sufficient if in official speeches he can express himself convincingly, in social intercourse intelligibly and truly.

Crassus insists upon the point that the perfect orator must be able to express himself on every subject with understanding, sound arrangement, and elegance: he alone then can be an orator who is well versed in all the accomplishments which befit a free man. Scaevola doubts whether such an orator actually exists. Antonius attempts to reconcile both opinions, maintaining that a knowledge of divers arts and sciences is a valuable ornament for an orator, not an absolute necessity. In that case, replies Crassus, an art of oratory is either null or utterly unimportant. Nature creates the orator. What is usually called rhetoric has never formed an orator where natural endowment and practice were wanting. But no one ever yet became an orator by nature and practice only without possessing material on which he could speak, and this, in the case of the complete orator, embraces the whole field of what is worth knowing.

Antonius agrees that this holds good of the ideal orator; but he wishes the conversation upon what belongs to an orator to confine itself to what is understood in common parlance under the term *orator*. For such it suffices that he be able to express himself on his subject clearly, appropriately, and elegantly, even supposing he has in the first place to take an opinion upon particular subjects of which he has no knowledge, as for instance the opinion of a jurist upon law.

"You mean a sort of journeyman orator,"* says Crassus. "Very well, to-morrow morning you can expound your views of what such an orator has to do and to learn."

In the introduction to the *Second Book* Cicero gives his brother a short sketch of the two principal characters in the discourse, Crassus and Antonius. Crassus did not repudiate the higher education which he owed to Greece, while preferring native learning to foreign; while Antonius was fain to pose as though not conversant with the Greeks at all.

With this Cicero proceeds in his report of the conversation. Scaevola had already left the com-

---

* operarium oratorem, § 263.

pany the day before; but his place was taken by Q. Catulus and C. Julius Caesar, to whom Scaevola had already communicated the previous day's conversation. Antonius takes the lead in the discourse, and speaks first of the material for rhetoric, which he says is either general and indefinite or special and definite. For the public speaker two kinds of oratory are the most important, judicial and deliberative (*genus iudiciale et deliberativum*), the third, less necessary, is the epideictic (*genus demonstrativum*),* which comprises eulogy, censure, warning, consolation, and the like, to which also belongs historical exposition. The first business of the orator is the invention of his material (*inventio*) which enables him to instruct, to enlist on his side, and to rouse his hearers (*docere, conciliare, movere*).

In an episode Caesar treats the head of wit, satire, and humour in their significance for the orator.

Antonius next discusses the arrangement of material (*dispositio*), which in judicial oratory includes

---

* *V.* Prof. Wilkins, de orat. i. p. 52 (Introd.). This division was first made by Aristotle.

the following sub-divisions: the opening (*exordium*), the exposition of the facts (*narratio*), the statement of the points at issue (*partitio ; causa ponatur, in quo videndum est quid in controversiam veniat*);* the establishment, and the refutation of the adverse positions (*confirmatio et refutatio ; suggerenda sunt fundamenta causae coniuncte et infirmandis contrariis et tuis confirmandis*);† finally the conclusion (*conclusio*). To this is appended a short discussion upon the views to be considered respecting the other two kinds of oratory. The third concern of the orator is the committing to memory, and with precepts for this the second book closes.

The *Third Book* Cicero introduces with a short lament over the sad fate of most of the participators in the discourse, and continues the account of the conversation.

In the afternoon of the same day the investigation respecting the orator is resumed in the shade of a neighbouring wood. Crassus takes up the

---

* 331.   † ib

discourse. He treats first of the oral form or expression (*de elocutione*), and lays down the demand that the orator shall speak good Latin (*Latine*), clearly (*plane*), fitly and tastefully (*apte et ornate*). The right use of rhetorical figures and rhythm contributes to beauty. He closes with the doctrine of delivery, on which in the end everything turns.

This principal work receives as it were a complement in two smaller and less important treatises, of which one, the *Brutus*, concerning famous orators (*Brutus sive de claris oratoribus*), gives a history of oratory, the other, the Orator (*Orator sive de optimo dicendi genere*), presents the picture of an orator as Cicero conceived it. The *Brutus*, dedicated to Marcus Brutus, was composed U.C. 708, B.C. 46. In the introduction Cicero laments the death of the great orator Hortensius:

Still, he esteems the deceased happy in not having lived to witness the time when the forum, which had been the theatre of his talents, lay bereft of its splendour and desolate. At this point the occasion which led to the discourse is related.

Atticus and Brutus had once visited Cicero at his Tusculan villa. They were wishing to shake off political anxieties, and divert themselves by instructive conversation. Atticus proposed that Cicero should take up again the discussion which he had lately held with him upon the origin of oratory, upon orators and their works. Cicero professes himself ready, and begins with a short account of oratory and its theory as it existed among the Greeks.

He then passes on to the history of Roman orators, which he brings down to his own time, and concludes by depicting his own course of study, and his endeavours after oratory, and requesting Brutus, in spite of the unfavourableness of the times, not to flag in his zeal for oratory, and to raise himself above the common run of advocates. Cicero in his otherwise pertinent criticism on the old Roman orators, cannot be altogether acquitted of a certain partiality in painting their achievements in much too glowing colours.

In this he probably had the intention of combating the prejudices of his contemporaries against the older orators, and of calling their attention to the treasures which they left lying unimproved.

He himself owns (*Brut.* § 123): "We have certainly done some good for our youth in teaching them to speak in a more stately and ornate style than before; but in this, perhaps, have done harm, that most of them have ceased, after my speeches, to read those of the ancients; on my own part, this is not so, since I always prefer them to my own." Upon which Brutus exclaims: "Count me also among the majority, although you have now made me aware that there is much that I need to read which I formerly despised."

Somewhat later than the *Brutus*, but still in the same year, was composed the *Orator sive de optimo dicendi genere*. This treatise likewise is dedicated to Brutus, who had himself put to Cicero the problem: "Whereas there prevails so great a difference amid good orators; what is the best type, *i.e.* the ideal of oratory?"

The orator, says Cicero, has to attend to three points: what to say, where, and how to say it. Touching briefly on the first two, Cicero has here almost exclusively to do with the *manner*; the question here is pre-eminently of what is fitting (τὸ πρέπον, *decorum*).

He starts with the proposition that for what is* plain, grand, or intermediate, an unpretentious, a weighty, an intermediate tone are respectively suitable (*parva summisse, modica temperate, magna graviter dicenda*).†

He determines the character of these three styles and gives rules for their employment.

As regards the form of the language, propriety shows itself in the choice of words, in the use of rhetorical figures, in the arrangement of the words, in the structure of sentences, and finally in the oratorical rhythm, the doctrine of which Cicero, following Isocrates amongst the Greeks, first ap-

---

* I borrow Dr. Sandys' words.
† § 101.

plied to Roman oratory. The treatise commends itself by ripe judgment and a pleasing presentation of the subject.

Cicero pronounces on it thus to his friend Lepta (*ad Fam.* vi. 18) :—

"I am highly delighted that my 'Orator' pleases you so much. It is my conviction that I have committed to it the entire results of any insight I have gained into the nature of eloquence. If it is what you say it seems to you, then I myself am good for something ; if not, I must reconcile myself to the fact that the reputation of my insight must suffer in just the same degree in which that of the book is impaired."

De partitione oratoria: Topica: de optimo genere oratorum.

Of slighter importance are the small treatises *De partitione oratoria sive partitiones oratoriae*, in the form of a catechism, in which Cicero answers in Latin the questions of his son Marcus on the principal doctrines of rhetoric, which he had previously propounded to him in Greek ; the *Topica*, the doctrine of the discovery of reasons and proof applied to procedure and supplemented by examples, drawn from judicial practice, written after the Topica of Aristotle from memory, during a voyage * U.C 710, B.C. 44, at the request of the famous jurist Trebatius, for whom the Greek original was too difficult. Lastly the tract *De optimo genere oratorum*, a preface to the translation of the two speeches of Aeschines and Demosthenes respectively against and for Ctesiphon, which Cicero had designed with a view to show by the best examples the real character of Attic eloquence, to which many Roman orators did not do justice.†

---

* Of eight days only, between Velia and Rhegium, 20th—28th July. Within the same days he wrote a fresh preface for his *de Gloria* : ad Att. xvi. 6: a notable feat of literary activity.

† Cp. n. above, p. 164, on the New Attic School.

CHAPTER V.

Cicero's Philosophical Works—Miscellaneous Work in Prose and Verse.

CICERO is entitled to special credit for having, in a series of writings, familiarised his countrymen with the doctrines of Greek philosophy, in fuller compass than any previous writer had done; and indeed he was less concerned to impart to them a bare historical knowledge of the Greek philosophers and their systems, than to regulate public and private life generally by philosophical principles. "Our whole discourse," says he in his treatise upon Laws (*de legg.* i. 62), "has for its aim the establishment of states and the improvement of nations."

The practical aim was supreme with him; hence he kept aloof from speculation, perhaps himself even feeling that he lacked the intuition, and the Roman people the understanding necessary for fathoming the depths of philosophy. What further drew him to

Greek philosophy was the beauty of its form, which his own taste enabled him to appreciate, and which he sought to turn to account for himself and his fellow-citizens. It was Plato in particular whom he held in view, in most of his dialogues, though in this respect he fell far beneath his model. His greatest service consists in his having been the first to adapt Roman speech for philosophical expression. He himself says (*Tusc.* ii. §§ 5-6) that as the Romans had become successful rivals of the Greeks in oratory, it was time, now that oratory was beginning to decline, for a philosophical literature also to be developed, which should rival that of Greece; then it would be possible to dispense with the Greek libraries. For this purpose he wished to incite educated Romans to express themselves on philosophical subjects also with method and understanding, as well as a due attention to the form of their composition.

For this reason he sets much less store by originality of philosophical research than by philosophical expression, which he contrasts with that of oratory. In the preface to his treatise on Duties (*de Off.* i. §§ 2, 3) he writes to his son Marcus: "In reading my writings, which do not very much dissent from the Peripatetics, you will use your own judgment as to their contents: to that I make no objection: but in your command of Latin expression you will certainly improve by the study of my writings. . . . I therefore urge you strongly to read diligently not only my speeches, but also my philosophical writings, which now are of nearly equal extent with them; for if in the former there is greater force of expression, the uniform and temperate style too should not be neglected."

After translations of several writings of Greek philosophers, Cicero brought out an independent work of six books on the State (*De re publica Libri vi.*).

De re publica vi. (Somnium Scipionis).

"I wrote it," says he (*De Divin.* ii., § 3), "while I was still holding the helm of the state, a great subject and thoroughly appropriate for a philosopher, which was also taken in hand with great fulness by Plato, Aristotle, Theophrastus, and the whole school of the Peripatetics."

From his letters it appears that he was already at work upon it in the year U.C. 700, B.C. 54. He writes in this year to Atticus (iv. 16): "I have put the conversation on the state into the mouths of Africanus, (L. Furius) Philus, Laelius, and Manilius; and have introduced along with them the young men Q. Tubero and P. Rutilius, together with the two sons-in-law of Laelius, Scaevola and Fannius. . . . . I only pray I may complete my purpose, for, as you do not fail to observe, I have chosen a task of great extent and importance, and requiring much leisure, which is just what fails me at present." Several alterations in the plan delayed the conclusion, so that he issued the work only just before his journey to Cilicia, U.C. 703, B.C. 51.

The time of the dialogue is fixed before the death of Scipio, in the Feriae Latinae of the year U.C. 625, B.C. 129. If Cicero had Plato's Republic, as to its external form, before his eyes, it was not a philosophical ideal, like the Platonic state, but the Roman constitution, that he took for the model of the best form of polity; that is to say, the Roman constitution as it existed before the disturbances of the Gracchi, slightly idealised it is true, but here in part he is following Polybius. He had in view, not only public life, but also education and domestic morality. According to Macrobius's expression (*Somn. Scip.* i., 1), Plato arranged the state as it ought to be, Cicero described it as it was arranged by Rome's ancestors; both had the same main tendency, to show that no state can be governed without the utmost justice.

The work, except some fragments contained in Fathers of the Church and grammarians, and the conclusion, was lost until, in the year 1822, Angelo Mai recovered part of the whole in a palimpsest at the Vatican, and published it. The Dream of Scipio (*Somnium Scipionis*) has been preserved by Macrobius, who wrote a commentary upon it.

Cicero frames its conclusion in a like manner to the myth in Plato's Republic.

Scipio Africanus tells how having come to Africa as military tribune, under the consul Manilius, he visited King Masinissa, who was a great friend of his family. Masinissa received him in the most friendly manner as a grandson of P. Cornelius Scipio, and entertained him with splendid hospitality.

After they had conversed far into the night about the elder Africanus, Scipio retired to rest and soon sank into an extraordinarily deep sleep. In a dream Africanus appeared to him, and thus reassured him in his terror: "Fear not, Scipio, but heed and record what I shall tell thee. Seest thou that city, which, subjugated to the Roman people by me, is now renewing the old war, and cannot rest? Thou art now serving in the siege almost as a common soldier; in two years, as consul, thou shalt destroy it, and win for thyself by thine own deeds the surname of honour which thou already holdest as a heritage from me. After thou hast destroyed Carthage, celebrated a triumph, attained the censorship, hast traversed Egypt, Syria, Asia, and Greece as an ambassador, thou wilt a second time be chosen consul, wilt destroy Numantia, and bring to its end a terrible war.

"Then when in thy chariot thou hast ridden up the Capitol, thou wilt find the state confounded by the counsels of my grandson;* here shalt thou shed the light of thy mind, thy insight and thy wisdom upon thy fatherland. But as I foresee the path of thy fate at that point branches off two ways; . . . the senate and all loyal citizens, the allies and the Latins will fix their gaze on thee and thy great name. On thee alone will rest the salvation of the state. In short, thou wilt have as dictator to set the republic on a firmer base, if so be that thou escape the impious hands of thy kindred. . . . . .

"That thou mayest the more ardently devote thyself to the defending of the state, know that for all who have preserved, strengthened, and made great their country, a special place is assured in heaven where they shall enjoy in blessedness an eternal life. For know that to the supreme God that rules the whole universe, nothing of all that is done on the earth is more acceptable than those banded unions

---

* Tib. Gracchus.

of men knit together by justice, which we call states. From Him have the leaders and saviours of these issued, and to Him do they return." (Somn. Scip. §§ 3-5.)

Scipio asks, whether Africanus himself and Paulus, his own father, and the rest, whom men deem dead, are still alive. "Yes," says Africanus, " all these are living, who have escaped from the bonds of the body as from prison. Your so-called life is death. Look, thy father Africanus is approaching."

On catching sight of him, Scipio shed a flood of tears; his father having embraced and kissed him, calmed him, and Scipio recovering utterance, says: " My noble, my hallowed father, since this is life, as I have heard from Africanus, why should I tarry on earth instead of coming hither to you?" "That," replied Paulus, "thou mayst not do: for until God, whose is this whole domain which thou beholdest, have set thee free from the prison of thy body, entrance hither remains closed against thee. Men are created for the purpose of tending the globe which thou seest here in the midst of the universe, and which thou callest the earth. And their souls spring from those eternal fires which ye call stars, which animated with a divine mind, in spherical form, traverse with wondrous swiftness their circular orbits.

"Thou, therefore, Publius, even as all the pious, must still keep the soul in the bonds of the body, and mayst not migrate from this earthly life without the command of Him by whom it was given thee, lest ye should seem to have deserted the post which has been assigned thee as a man by God.

"Rather, Scipio, like thy grandfather here and me thy sire, practise justice and pious duty, which binding as it is in regard to parents and kindred, is most binding in regard to thy country. Such a life is the way to heaven and to the ranks of those who have lived their life, and released from the body inhabit this place which thou beholdest." That place was the Milky Way beaming forth in purest light amid its flaming stars, from whence Scipio overlooked the whole universe; and, when he lowered his gaze to the earth, it appeared to him so small, and the mighty Roman Empire on it such a mere speck, that he was thoroughly discontented with his insignificance. Then said Africanus: "Raise your eyes again and behold those lofty domains." And he showed him the nine celestial spheres; the outermost which encircles and holds together the others, and in which the fixed stars are fastened; then the seven circles of the planets, Saturn, Jupiter, Mars, the Sun, Venus, Mercury, and the Moon. Lastly, ninth and nethermost, the earth, the realm of mortals, where only the souls of men are immortal. At the same time Scipio perceived the music which the seven* spheres rang out in their revolution, and which the human ear is too dull to catch. Again Scipio turned his gaze upon the earth. Africanus showed him its five zones, of which two only, the temperate, are inhabited, while only over a limited ortion of the northern one sounds the name of Rome. "And even those who speak of you, how

---

* There are seven tones, answering to the notes of the heptachord: but *eight* spheres produce them, Mercury and Venus, however, giving the same tone.

long will they speak of you? And what is an earthly year compared with that world-year, of which since Romulus' death not even the twentieth part has passed away! Thou seest how empty is human renown, how meagre the reward it offers. 'Tis virtue alone that by her allurements must lead thee to true honour; ask not for human renown, which is limited by space and time, and transitory like all that is of earth.

"Strive ever after that which is higher, and cherish the conviction that thy body, not thyself, is mortal. For not this thy visible form is thyself, but the soul, the deity within thee which there lives and feels, remembers and anticipates, and moves, sways, and governs the body even as the Supreme Deity does the world. Only that which for ever moves itself is eternal; what is moved is dead as soon as it ceases to be moved. Motion is the primal principle which has no beginning, and our soul is therefore eternal because motion is its nature and peculiar essence. And the worthiest motion for it is the activity which is directed to the welfare of the fatherland, and the more it moves and exercises itself therein, the more easily will it soar up to this heavenly realm and its proper home, and that the more speedily if, even while it was pent in the body, it ever strove forth, intent upon releasing itself as far as possible from the body. But the souls of those who have given themselves up to bodily pleasures, and enslaved as it were to these, at the instigation of passions responsive to no call save that of pleasure, violate the laws of gods and men—such souls roam around the earth when they quit the body, and return not to this place until many centuries of wanderings have been fulfilled." (§§ 6-21 in substance.)

Africanus vanished, and Scipio forthwith awoke out of his sleep.

As in Plato, the treatise on laws (*De Legibus*) connects itself with the *Republic*; Cicero, however, in it follows the principles of the Stoics, and appears in particular to have kept in view the work of Chrysippus Περὶ νόμων. Of this as originally planned, covering five books at least, probably as much as six, only three

De Legibus.

are extant. The form is that of dialogue, conducted by Cicero himself on the one part, his brother Quintus and Atticus on the other. The treatise is nowhere alluded to by Cicero, and, as it appears incomplete, was probably not given to the world till after his death, while it must have been composed directly after the *De re publica,* as Cicero himself sets it in a certain connexion with the latter. "Whereas," says he (§ 20), "the settled form of government which Scipio in those six books has set forth as the best, must be maintained and defended by us, and all laws rendered conformable to that kind of constitution, I purpose to trace the radical notion of right from nature, which must be our guide in this whole investigation." The first book contains the principles of right (*principia iuris*), the second treats of divine rights (*de legibus divinis*), the third of human laws, emanating from the authorities (*de legibus magistratuum*), which from its significant contents is especially important for the study of Roman law.

Cicero in the two treatises just named applied philosophy to politics; later on domestic and political circumstances impelled him to the composition of treatises, some of a practically philosophical, and some of a systematic character. Caesar's dictatorship terminated his political activity; he retired almost wholly from public life, and almost exclusively applied himself to philosophy. The greater and the most important part of his philosophical writings belong to the period U.C. 708-10 (B.C. 46-44).

The extraordinary fertility which Cicero evinced in the latter years of his life, disturbed as they were by domestic unhappiness and political anxieties, is explicable only on the assumption that he had previously amassed the material for his works. He himself writes to Atticus (xii. 52) : "You will ask, 'How do you manage to compose as you are doing?' I have the materials in notebooks (ἀπόγραφα),* and

---

* Or better, "they are copies (from Greek originals)," frank assertion of the fact that "Cicero's philosophical works are in substance translations, though free translations, from Greek originals," *v.* Dr. Reid *Academics*, p. 26. At the same time in one of his works (*de off.* i. § 6) he claims to be more than a mere translator.

that lightens the labour; I have merely to clothe them in words, and these flow freely."

Beside these he had stored up a collection of introductions (*volumen prooemiorum*), and out of these he chose one suited to each respective treatise, whence it once happened that from forgetfulness he used one introduction for two different works.* In the year U.C. 708, B.C. 46, were composed the *Paradoxa ad M. Brutum*, dissertations upon six leading Stoic maxims, forming,

Paradoxa:
Consolatio, Hortensius,
Academicorum iv.

as Cicero states in the introduction, specimens of exercises, as he used to compose them, when he treated the so-called school-theses in rhetorical fashion. The six maxims are:—The moral good (τὸ καλόν) is the only good. Virtue suffices in itself for a happy life. All wrong actions are equal, and likewise all right actions. Every unwise man is mad. The wise alone is free, the unwise a slave. The wise man alone is rich.

The death of his beloved daughter Tullia, U.C. 709,

---

* *V.* note supr. p. 189.

B.C. 45,* gave rise to the discourse on consolation, or the mitigation of grief (*Consolatio sive de luctu minuendo*), based upon Crantor's Περὶ πένθους. He writes to Atticus (xii. 14): "My grief will yield to no consolation. I have even done that which no one has done before me, have addressed to myself written consolation. I will send you the book as soon as my amanuenses have made a copy of it." Elsewhere we find: "My *Consolation* exerts a very salutary influence upon myself, and I believe it will in many cases prove useful to others." (*De Divin.* ii. § 3.) We possess only scattered fragments of this discourse.

The dialogue *Hortensius*, composed in the same year, was intended to serve as an introduction to systematic philosophy.

As Cicero himself says, he intended by this treatise to exhort strongly to the study of philosophy (*De divin.* ii. § 1) by refuting the objections alleged against it. (*Tusc.* ii. § 4.) The treatise, which we

---

* Cp. the beautiful letter of Ser. Sulpicius, ad Fam. iv. 5.

no longer possess, was highly prized in antiquity. It was upon reading this that St. Augustine applied himself to philosophy.

The *Hortensius* was succeeded in the same year by the *Academica*, in four books (*Academicorum libri iv.*), in which he carefully develops all that can be said on behalf of the Academy (*Tusc.* ii. § 4), and shows what style is suited to philosophy, and what is most consistent therewith and in best taste.*

The treatise originally consisted of two dialogues, the Catulus and the Lucullus. On the request of the learned M. Terentius Varro to play a part in a Ciceronian treatise, Cicero re-wrote the work, and divided the subject into four books (*ad Att.* xiii. 13-19). Besides the dedication to Varro† we possess the first book of the second issue (*Academica posteriora*), and the second of the first (*Academica priora*). The former contains the conversation of Cicero and Varro in presence of Atticus at Cicero's estate at Cumae. Varro undertakes to expound the

---

* de divin. ii. § 1.
† ad fam. ix 8.

views of the Old Academy. He begins with Socrates, then passes on to Plato, the founder of the Academy, and gives a survey of his ethics, physics, and dialectic. In opposition to the Platonic doctrine of ideas Aristotle arises, and the principle of the Platonic ethics, that happiness consists in virtue, is refuted by Theophrastus. Strato, the disciple of the latter, leaves ethics on one side, and confines himself to physics.

The followers of Plato are Speusippus and Xenocrates; these are succeeded by Polemo, Crates, and Crantor. The disciples of Polemo were Zeno and Arcesilas. The former gives to ethics, physics, and dialectic the specific direction which the Stoic school followed. Cicero now takes up the conversation, exhibiting the system of Arcesilas. The latter declares that we can know nothing, but that everything is involved in obscurity. His is styled the New Academic School, but Cicero is of opinion that as in its principle of knowledge it does not substantially diverge from Plato, it ought still to be included in the older school. The conversation here breaks off. In the *second book*, entitled *Lucullus*, Lucullus, Hortensius, Catulus, and Cicero are the disputants. Lucullus brings forward the opinion of Antiochus of the reality of our impressions, which Cicero in the spirit of the New Academy, which allows the probability only of our impressions, proceeds to contest.*

De finibus v.
Tuscul. Disput. v.

The five books *De Finibus bonorum et malorum*, dedicated to Brutus, occupy a leading position among his systematic writings. The work, projected some time before (*De leg.* i. § 52), was completed likewise in U.C. 709, B.C. 45. Cicero expresses himself upon the purpose of the work to the following effect (*De Divin.* ii. § 2): "Since the foundation of philosophy depends on the view taken of the highest good and evil, I cleared up this question in five books, so that it might appear what each philosopher has to say

---

* "The *Academica* was composed of two long fragments of Antiochus taken from different works, two of Philo from the same work, four of Clitomachus from three or four different works. No attempt was made to recast or arrange the subject matter. . . . Cicero merely set the fragments in the framework of the dialogue. The local scenery, the illustrations from Roman history and the connecting-links, constitute all that is due to his own invention." Reid *Acad.* p. 53. Cp. n. supr. p. 203.

on the subject, and what may be urged against him." The question which here offers itself for treatment he propounds in his introduction to the first book (§ 11): "What is the aim, the supreme and ultimate end, to which all our endeavours after happiness and well-doing must tend? What must nature pursue as the highest of all desirable goods? What must she shun as the greatest evil?" As Cicero wished to discuss with accuracy the divergent views of philosophers he divided the subject into three dialogues, giving each a distinct garb, while nevertheless himself retaining the leading part in each.

The subordinate characters are of persons dead at the time of writing. The *first dialogue*, which treats of the views of the Epicureans, comprises Books i., ii., and is supposed to take place U.C. 704, B.C. 50. L. Manlius Torquatus and C. Valerius Triarius taking part in it. Cicero gives a criticism upon the physical system of the Epicureans, which differs not materially from that of Democritus; then of the Epicurean logic, which he calls unarmed and open to attack as knowing nothing of definition, divisions, or conclusions; but placing perception simply in the senses and therefore wavering with them in the determination of the truth. The ethics, moreover, of the Epicureans start from the false principle that pleasure is the only and the highest thing we pursue, and pain the one thing which we have to avoid.

With this all virtue, all self-sacrifice for others, in short all that ennobles man, is renounced, and bodily comfort, which is common to man with the beasts, alone remains as the highest goal of happiness. Torquatus defends the views of the Epicureans respecting the highest good. The pursuit of enjoyment is proper to every creature. Man seeks the pleasure not only of the body, but also of the soul. Therefore the wise strives after virtue, and often purchases the enjoyment of the soul by the sacrifice of a lesser pleasure or by the voluntary endurance of some pain. While requiring the pleasure of the soul he does not renounce those sensuous enjoyments which promote the comfort of the body. The Epicurean therefore disregards logic, because it contributes nothing to comfort; but not so physics, because the observation and study of nature free him from the false fears and superstition which destroy the repose of life.

In the Second Book Cicero proves the untenableness of these views.

The highest good must be such as in and for itself, all advantage or reward apart, is praiseworthy and to be pursued. That, however, is not pleasure or enjoyment, but virture. The truly wise will rather be a Hercules amidst a host of pains and sorrows, than an Epicurus in satiety of pleasures.

The *second dialogue*, comprising Books iii., iv., introduces Cato and Cicero conversing in the year U.C. 702, B.C. 52. Cato sets forth the ethics of the Stoics, which rest on the principle that virtue is the highest good, vice the greatest evil. Man attains happiness when he lives conformably to nature, and in this wisdom consists.

The Fourth Book contains Cicero's rejoinder. The ethics of the Stoics only verbally diverge from those of the Academics and Peripatetics.

In the point wherein it differs from these, it too is open to attack, namely in allowing no difference amid virtues and vices, while it declares pain to be not an evil (*malum*), but a hardship (*asperum*), which, however, exerts no influence on happiness. The sufferer for all that feels the pain no less, be it hardship or evil. The error of the Stoics lies in their attempting to combine two contrary principles: the good is a moral good alone and the craving for that which contributes to happiness is a natural impulse.*

The *third dialogue*, Book v., is fixed at the time of Cicero's first sojourn at Athens, U.C. 675, B.C. 79.

---

* In Tusc. v. 21 sq. Cic. goes further: and maintains that a life of virtue is not only happy, but the happiest possible, in spite of inconsistency with de fin. iv. § 60 (*ib.* § 32). The words that follow are significant of Cicero's disregard of philosophical consistency: "You try to bind me by the letter of my former statements: that will do in the case of others who have to conform to self-imposed conditions in their discussions; but we live from one day to the next: whatever has struck us by its probability, we say. So we alone are free." (*ib.* § 33.) We are reminded of a similar reply of Cic. to a charge of *political* inconsistency, *Cluent.* § 139: "It would be a great mistake for anyone to suppose that he has in our forensic speeches an authentic record of our opinions. They are all the utterance of a particular case and a particular time."

Besides himself, his brother Quintus, his cousin L. Cicero, Atticus, and M. Pupius Piso, take part in it. The last-named unfolds the ethical principles of the older Academics and the Peripatetics, who, like the Stoics, regard virtue as the highest good, but withal take into account accidental evils and sufferings in their estimate of a happy life. Hence he explains that he has no hesitation in maintaining that all wise men are invariably happy, but it is possible that one may be happier than another.

Cicero followed up this treatise with the Tusculan disputations, in five books (*Tusculanarum Disputationum libri v.*), U.C. 710, B.C. 44; which work likewise is dedicated to Brutus.

"It was intended to show what is chiefly necessary for a happy life; to which end the first book treats of the contempt of death, the second of the endurance of pain, the third of the alleviation of sorrow, the fourth of other disturbances of the mind. The fifth book embraces a theme which glorifies philosophy generally; that virtue in itself suffices for happiness." (*De Divin.* ii. § 2.)

Apart from his philosophical aim Cicero intended also to show by examples how the treatment of philosophical questions might be combined with practice in oratory. On this he himself speaks in the introduction to the first book: "I have always deemed a perfect philosophy to be one that could treat of the greatest questions with fulness and finish. So zealously have I devoted myself to the practice of this that I have even ventured to give scholastic lectures (*scholas*) after the fashion of the Greeks. I lately tried my powers in this line at my Tusculan villa, where several friends of mine had met. As formerly I used to declaim in imaginary causes, a practice which no one has followed longer than myself, so now in my old age I find practice for declamation in this. I asked someone to state a thesis which he would like to hear discussed, and then treated it, sitting or walking about. I have thus arranged in five books the 'schools' (in the Greek sense) of five days. The plan was for him who wished to hear a discussion to state his own views; and for me then to speak on the other side.

"This, as you know, is the old Socratic method of peaking in opposition to the opinion of another; Socrates thought it the easiest way of arriving at at was the nearest approach to positive truth.' (§§ 7, 8.)

The occasionally careless form of expression may very likely arise from the attempt to reproduce the immediate interchange of ideas. The treatise was amongst the most widely read of Cicero's works.

Next come the three books *De natura deorum iii.: de divinatione ii.. de fato.* upon the existence of the gods (*de natura deorum libri iii.*), published in the same year. We have it not quite complete, as several sections are wanting towards the end of Bk. III. Like the preceding, this work is dedicated to Brutus. Greek treatises are employed, those in particular of Phaedrus, Chrysippus, and Carneades. The book is in dialogue form. In the Feriae Latinae of some year between U.C. 676-679, B.C. 78-75, Cicero, coming to Cotta, an adherent of the Academy, finds at his house C. Velleius, then the leading connoisseur in the Epicurean philosophy, and

Lucilius Balbus, who was so well versed in the writings of the Stoics as to be able to hold his own in this field with the most famous Greeks.

The subject of the conversation was the being of the gods, a subject which to Cotta appeared highly obscure, and on which he wanted to hear the views of Velleius and Balbus. Velleius propounds the view of the Epicureans. Gods do exist: the innate idea[*] universal, though dim, which men have of the gods testifies to this. According to this idea or intuition the gods are immortal and blessed. Blessed the gods can only be because they never either themselves experience any distress nor bring it upon other beings.

They are therefore free from aversion and partiality, for these are weaknesses, which pertain not to a perfect being.

In the perfection of the gods consists the reason why we ought not indeed to fear, but to revere them. Fear set aside, all superstition is also set aside.

---

[*] πρόληψις (*anticipatio*).

As to the form of the gods, it can only be human, because that is the most beautiful and at the same time that in which a reasonable soul has its abode. The gods, however, have no body, but only *something like a body which is not apprehended by the senses. The life of the gods is most blessed: it passes in continuous inaction, in the enjoyment of their wisdom and virtue, and in the consciousness of the eternal duration of their pleasures.

Against this view Cotta protests: he maintains that there are gods, not indeed on the ground partly inconclusive, partly false of a universal intuition of them.

If there are gods, the question for us is to know whence and where they are, and how constituted. If the gods, as the Epicureans hold, have like all else originated from atoms, then they cannot be eternal and consequently cannot be blessed. They are, however, as Velleius says, not bodies, but something like bodies. But that is only an evasion, for what this "something like a body" is we have no conception. The human

---

* quasi corpus, § 49. simile corporis, § 75.

form which Epicurus assigns them has been attributed to them also by poets and artists. The human form appears to man, it is true, the most beautiful, but it does not follow from this that there cannot be a more beautiful, and that it alone can be the domicile of reason and virtue and consequently of happiness. Besides, what have the gods to do with the limbs of the human form, as they do not use them seeing they have nothing to do? Further Epicurus' argument for their immortality is null, namely that the principle of equipoise (ἰσονομία, *aequilibrium*) requires an immortal beside the mortal nature.

Also their gods cannot be blessed, since blessedness without virtue or virtue without activity cannot be imagined, whereas the Epicurean gods are eternally idle, in fact they cannot even enjoy the pleasures of the body which Epicurus sets down as the highest good. The absence of pain and mere consciousness of blessedness is by itself no blessedness. The reverence which the Epicureans claim for the gods, they themselves do away with; for we have no reason to honour idle gods who do not care for or help men.

In the *Second Book* Balbus expounds the doctrine of the Stoics. He first proves that there are gods from the consentient belief of all mankind, from the manifestations of the gods, from predictions and oracles, and especially from the adaptation of means to ends in the world and its constitution as a whole and in detail.

Human intelligence can only be derived from a Divine Intelligence, and since there cannot exist anything better than the universe nor be conceived, and there is nothing better than reason, therefore there must be a Reason ruling in the universe, and in fact all parts of the universe are in such harmony that they can be held together only by a Divine Spirit. Beside our world a divinity must be attributed to the heavenly bodies on account of their voluntary motion, order, and uniformity. The gods reign over the universe because they are gods, because all is subject to that which thinks, because the admirable relation of means to end in heaven and earth points to a Ruling Intelligence. Above all, moreover, the gods care for mankind as a whole and individually.

The *Third Book* contains **Cotta's** reply. The popular opinion of the gods, of their manifestations and revelations, should not be advanced by any philosopher as an argument for their existence.

The universe, and the heavenly bodies likewise, cannot be gods, for they are bodies, but all bodies are liable to suffering, and therefore cannot be eternal or immortal.

The providential care of the gods for mankind is contradicted by the fact that much which they bestow, and often reason itself, harms men, and not seldom the most virtuous are the most unfortunate. The plea that the gods, like kings, cannot think of everything, that they concern themselves about the whole, not the individual, is absurd. Gods cannot, like men, excuse themselves on the ground of ignorance, and if they concern themselves for the whole, why do they suffer whole states and nations to perish? "This broadly," concludes Cotta, "is what I have to say about the being of the gods, not at all in order to undermine the belief in it, but that you may acknowledge how dark the problem is, and how hard it is to solve its perplexities." *

The two books on Divine Revelations (*De Divinatione libri ii.*) are, as Cicero intended them, to be regarded as a supplement to the treatise on the Being of the Gods.† The universal belief in divination, and the opinion of many philosophers, in particular the Stoics, as to the truth of it invite a minuter investigation, especially as divination is intimately connected with religion: that we may not fall victims either to an impious imposture or a childish superstition. Cicero reproduces a conversation which he had upon the subject with his brother Quintus, at the Tusculan villa. The latter had shortly before read the attack of Cotta on divination in the treatise on the being of the gods. The matter appears to him not yet to be settled, and he still feels bound to agree with the Stoics that divination does exist. He distinguishes two kinds of divination, the artificial, which foretells the future from the entrails of animals, from the

---

* *N. D.* iii. § 93.
† *De Divin.*, ii., 1.

flight of birds, from lightnings and other tokens, from the stars, and from lots: and the natural, in dreams and oracles. Not so much causes as events, he thought, were to be inquired into. The art of divination rests upon observations which men have made from primeval times, just as the physician knows by observation the healing power of certain herbs, and as one foretells the weather by certain prognostics.

Chance cannot reign here because chance never hits upon the truth exactly. Further, the objection that predictions have often not come to pass, does not hold. Signs of the weather, too, sometimes deceive, and healing simples not seldom disappoint. The truth of divination is best confirmed by the great multitude of instances of it handed down, of which Quintus gives a rich collection derived from Greek and Roman history.

The *Second Book* contains Cicero's reply, which is founded on the views of the Academics. No divination informs us of that which we can apprehend by the senses, or learn by any science or art: it only unfolds that which is remitted to chance, and which not even a god can know ; for what such a one knows must certainly happen, and then it ceases to be chance. But if one denies chance altogether, and ascribes everything to fate, what is the use of prediction, since one can never escape what is predestined ? It is on the contrary even harmful, as it spoils the enjoyment of the present.

The examples which Quintus cites are no proofs such as a philosopher requires, for he cannot refer such a question to witnesses who either tell the truth accidentally, or may, with evil purpose, falsify the truth, or lie outright. He must avail himself of rational proofs, and may not conclude from events, especially from such as are so open to doubt. The nullity of the different divinations is shown in their several varieties. Cicero was himself an augur all the same from U.C. 703, B.C. 51, and actually wrote a special book upon auguries (*De Auguriis*).

A dissertation (*de Fato*) followed as a complement to the two preceding works. It was produced shortly after the death of Caesar, U.C. 710, B.C. 44, at the request of Hirtius, and contained an investigation concerning the Stoic doctrine of fate. The beginning and the end of the work are lost, and the torso which is left us suffers from frequent lacunae and corruptions. Cicero appears to have given prominence to the contradictions between the freedom of the will and the postulate of fate.

De gloria: de Senectute: de Amicitia. In the same year, Cicero wrote, beside the work upon Renown (*de gloria*) in two books, now lost, but known to have been possessed by Petrarch, the two treatises, the *Cato* and the *Laelius*. The *Cato*, a dialogue on old age (*Cato sive de Senectute*), is dedicated to Atticus.

Cicero could offer him (so he writes in the introduction) no consolation as to the melancholy circumstances of their country; he therefore sought to alleviate for them both the common burden of old age. "The composition of this book," he goes on to say, " has afforded me so much pleasure, that it has not only effaced all the discomforts of old age, but made it easy and delightful. Philosophy then can never be praised as it deserves, since her votary can pass every time of life without discomfort."* Cicero represents a meeting of Scipio Africanus and Laelius with Cato, now at the age of 84, U.C. 604, B.C. 150, a year before the death of the latter. They express to him their surprise that he bears the discomforts of age so lightly.

"To such," he replies, "as have no resource in themselves for a good and happy life, every time of life is burdensome, but to those who seek for all good from themselves, nothing can appear an evil which natural necessity entails . . . Such wisdom as I have consists in following nature, the best of guides, as a deity, and obeying her, since it is not probable that having apportioned so well all the other parts of life, she has, like a slovenly playwright, neglected the last act. But it was inevitable that a last stage should come, a stage of wrinkles and decay like that which is seasonable in the ripeness of fruits and cereals, and a wise man must bear it contentedly. Fighting

---

* § 2.

against nature, what else is it than battling, like the giants, with the gods?" (§ 4, 5.)

He proceeds to meet the four chief charges, which men are wont to urge against old age: that it condemns men to inaction; that it is weak and decrepit; that it lacks pleasures; that it is close to death; and concludes with the hope of a future life: "If my belief in the immortality of the human soul be a delusion, it is a delusion I gladly indulge, a delusion which I would not have wrested from me while I live. And if, as some petty philosophers maintain, all sensation ends with death, then I have no fear that dead philosophers will mock my delusion."*

The *Laelius*, a conversation on friendship (*Laelius sive de Amicitia*), is also dedicated to Atticus, who had requested Cicero to write on the subject.

Its contents purport to be derived from the account which Q. Mucius Scaevola the augur had given to Cicero in his youth of the conversation of Laelius with his sons-in-law, the aforesaid Scaevola and C.

---

* § 86.

Fannius, shortly after the death of his friend Scipio Africanus minor, U.C. 625, B.C. 129.

The treatise engages us by its pleasing presentment and exhaustive treatment of the materials, which Cicero appears to have taken, partly from Theophrastus' treatise περὶ φιλίας.

He prefixes to it the maxim that friendship can only exist between the good. Friendship is unanimity of feeling on things human and divine, combined with reciprocal goodwill. Next after virtue and wisdom friendship is the choicest boon that the gods could give to men. Friend sees in friend as it were a copy of himself; for nature knits true friendship, which teaches us to love virtue in others even as in ourselves.

Friendship, therefore, which is grounded on self-interest is transitory, but that which is founded on virtue is eternal. It holds then as the first law between friends that they ask of one another nothing that is wrong, and the following maxims are false:—that every man must be disposed towards his friend as his friend is towards him; that friendship consists in an exactly equal interchange of services; that a man's friends must appraise him at the value which he sets upon himself; that a man should love his friend with a sense that one day he may come to hate him. If virtue knits friendships, the test of misfortune may be dispensed with; though Ennius* has well said :—

"A trusty friend in treacherous straits is proved."

The question whether new friends are to be preferred to old, hence answers itself.

Friendships, like wine, are mellowed by time, and the adage is right which says that friends, to be real friends, must have eaten many a peck of salt together.

Those only are worthy of friendship whom we are impelled to love not on external grounds, but for their own sake. As each one loves himself without expecting a return for it, so must we love our friends likewise; for the true friend is a sort of second self. Friends are one soul in two bodies. Friendship is given by nature as a supporter of virtue, not an abettor in vice.

Nothing is, therefore, more important than

---

* § 64.

the choice of a friend; here the principle holds good—test first, then love, not *vice versa*.

For nothing brings its own punishment so surely as the unfortunate choice of a friend; nature has created us for fellowship, nature knits friendship by truth and integrity; hence the dictum of Terence,

"Truth wins but hatred, complaisance a friend,"

is only half true. Let us see that complaisance does not degenerate into flattery, the worst curse which can befall a friendship; and let truth be free from bitterness and vituperation, then it does not produce hate. True friendship is not sundered even by death. "For me," says Laelius (§ 102), "Scipio lives, though he was so suddenly taken from me, and ever will live; for it was the man's virtue that I loved, and this is not annihilated. . . . . There is nothing amid all that fortune or nature has given me that I can compare with Scipio's friendship."

De officiis iii.

The three books upon Duties (*de officiis libri iii.*), to which the lost book upon the virtues (*de virtutibus*) was perhaps an appendix, close the series of philosophical writings

Cicero completed them in the last months of the year U.C. 710, B.C. 44,* and dedicated them to his son Marcus, to whom he sent the work at Athens, where he was engaged in the study of philosophy, under the guidance of the Peripatetic Cratippus. In his doctrine of moral duties he principally follows the Stoics; *i.e.* in the first two books he was guided by the work of Panaetius περὶ τοῦ καθήκοντος; still, as he himself says, he has not been a mere translator, but, of his own judgment and choice, has drawn from Greek sources as far as appeared to him most desirable.

The doctrine of duties falls with him into two portions: a theoretical, the doctrine of the highest good; and a practical, with which alone he is here concerned.

In every one of our actions a twofold question is involved: whether it is morally good (*honesta*) or expedient (*utilis*).

Morally good actions admit of comparison with one another as to preferableness, as likewise do expedient actions; and finally that which is morally

---

* *ad Att.* xv. 31; xvi. 11.

good may come into competition with the expedient.

The doctrine of duty falls into three chief divisions accordingly. The *first book* treats of the morally good in itself, and of the conflict of alternatives when it is applied to conduct; the *second book* treats of the expedient, wherein the principle holds that the morally good is likewise the expedient; the *third* treats of the conflict between moral rectitude and expediency, a department which Panaetius in his treatise upon duty had entirely passed over.* Strictly speaking such a conflict is not possible, for whatever is not moral is also inexpedient; still in everyday life many cases of collision do occur.

Here it holds good as a universal rule: what is held to be expedient cannot be morally wrong, or if it really is wrong it can no longer be held to be expedient.

---

* "The third book, in which Cic. especially prides himself on his greater self-dependence, is undoubtedly the most defective of all in treatment." (Dr. Holden, introd. de off. xxxix.) He consulted for it a work of Posidonius, pupil of Panaetius, and an essay of Hekaton of Rhodes. A leading charm of the whole work is its wealth of illustration from Roman history: e.g. the case of Regulus in book iii.

Cicero essayed his powers as a writer in other fields of prose also.

Thus he had commenced, Quintilian informs us (xii. 3.10), a work on the Systematic Exposition of the Civil Law (*De iure civili in artem redigendo*).

Other miscellaneous works in prose and verse.

The account of his Political Life (*ratio* or *expositio consiliorum suorum*), not published until after his death, denoted by him in his letters to Atticus as private memoirs (ἀνέκδοτα), was of import for political history. He had written in Greek a memoir (ὑπόμνημα) of his consulate.

In U.C 694, B.C. 60, he sent the book to Atticus with the remark: "If there is anything in it which to your *Attic* taste seems bad Greek or unclassical, I will not put forward the plea that Lucullus made to you about his book, that he had introduced here and there a few barbarisms and solecisms, to show that the history was the work of a Roman. No, if there is any such slip in my work, it will be without my knowledge and against my will."*

---

* ad Att. i. 19, after Prof. Tyrrell.

In another letter to Atticus (ii. 1) he says: "My book has used up the whole pomade-box of Isocrates, the paint-boxes of all his school, and a touch of Aristotle's rouge to boot. . . . Posidonius has already written to me from Rhodes, that when he read my memoir, which I sent to him that he might treat the same subject with greater grace, far from being encouraged to write, he was positively overawed by the task. In a word, I have struck consternation into the Greek people. So much so that those who used to pester me to give them something to polish up, have ceased to annoy me." Mention is made also of a book by him on Remarkable Things,* and one upon geography, under the title of Chorographia.

To Cicero's original works must be added his translations from the Greek authors.

His procedure in translation he describes in the following terms (*de opt. gen. orat.* § 14):—

"I have translated the most famous speeches of the two great orators among the Attics, not in inter-

---

* *Admiranda*, Plin. N. H. xxxi. 8-2.

preter fashion, but as an orator, keeping the sentences the same, and also the mould in which they are cast, but adapting the words to the idiom of our own language; and there I have not thought it necessary to translate word for word, but have only kept up the main sense and character of the words employed; for I thought it my duty to weigh them out to the reader, not to count them out." Besides the two speeches of Aeschines and Demosthenes against and for Ctesiphon, he translated Xenophon's Oeconomicus, while still a young man (*De Off.* ii. 87); also Plato's Protagoras and Timaeus, the latter, as appears from the introduction to the considerable fragment of the translation still preserved, after writing the *Academica*.

Cicero also tried his hand at poetry, though not with especial success, to conclude at least from the unfavourable judgments of the Roman writers upon his poetical performances; for the scanty fragments of his poetry that remain scarcely allow us to judge. Beside several other writings, such as the *Pontius Glaucus*, according to Plutarch (*vit. Cic.* ii.) a work of his boyhood, *Alcyones, Uxorius, Nilus, Limon,* an elegy and epigrams, he wrote *Marius*, an epic; also a poem upon his consulate (*de Consulatu Suo*) in three books, and one upon his reverses (*de temporibus suis*), likewise in three books. From the *Marius* he himself has preserved a fragment (*de Divin.* i. § 106), an excellent description of an augury, also a longer fragment out of the second book upon his consulate (*ib.* i. §§ 17-22), which is conceived quite in the style of Ennius. Quintilian (xi. i. 24) rightly censures in this epic the self-glorification of the writer, and the ridiculous introduction of the gods. "If he had only in his poems forborne from the passage which spiteful critics are never weary of attacking :—

    'Yield, arms! to gown, bay-wreath to civic praise.'

    ' How fortunate a natal day was thine
       In that proud consulate, O Rome, of mine!' *

'The Jupiter who calls him to the council-chamber of the gods,' 'The Minerva who instructed him in all arts'; for such liberties he has allowed himself

---

* "Cedant arma togae, concedat laurea laudi. O fortunatam natam me consule Romam." (For the translation, which is Gifford's, *v.* Mayor, Juv. x. 122.)

after certain examples among the Greeks." As a young man Cicero translated from the Greek the Phaenomena and the Prognostica of Aratus, of which noteworthy fragments have been preserved.*

Lastly he has borrowed several passages from Homer and the Greek tragedians, in cases in which he required in his writings quotations from poets which no Latin authors afforded him, as for instance in *De Divin.* ii., §§ 63-64, Tusc. ii., §§ 20-25.

Cicero's younger brother Quintus—U.C. 652-711, B.C. 102-43—was also an author. When legatus of Caesar in Gaul, U.C. 700, B.C. 54, he wrote while in winter quarters four tragedies in sixteen days, probably translations from Greek originals.

He was also an epic poet, and his Annals, men-

---

* It is surely no mean testimony to Cicero's versatile genius, that Lucretius should have frequently imitated the "Aratea," and that (if Jerome is to be trusted) Cicero should, after the poet's death, have been charged with the task of editing his great poem. Not that Cic. is likely to have made any material corrections in it. In Cic.'s own poems 'we observe the entire lack of inspiration combined with considerable smoothness.' They mark a distinct stage in the development of the Latin hexameter. (Munro, Lucr., introd.; Cruttwell Hist. R. Lit, p. 186.)

tioned by Cicero,* were probably in epic form. Besides three letters of his, which are extant (*ad Fam.* xvi., 8, 16, 26), there is also the despatch to his brother Marcus U.C. 690, B.C. 64, about his candidature for the consulship, *de petitione consulatus ad M. Tullium fratrem:* advice as to the most successful method of canvass.

---

* *ad Att.* ii. 16.

www.ingramcontent.com/pod-product-compliance
Lightning Source LLC
Chambersburg PA
CBHW020756230426
43666CB00007B/712